PATH TO THE LIGHT

Kabbalah Centre Publishing is a registered DBA of Kabbalah Centre International, Inc.

For further information:

The Kabbalah Centre
155 E. 48th St., New York, NY 10017
1062 S. Robertson Blvd., Los Angeles, CA 90035

1.800.Kabbalah www.kabbalah.com

Printed in USA, July 2019

ISBN: 978-1-57189-974-3

eBook ISBN: 978-1-57189-987-3

Design: HL Design (Hyun Min Lee) www.hldesignco.com

PATH TO THE LIGHT

KABBALAH CENTRE PUBLISHING

DECODING THE BIBLE WITH KABBALAH

An Anthology
of Commentary
from Kabbalist
Rav Berg

**BOOK OF
BERESHEET**
Volume 4

Miketz
Vayigash
Vayechi

The study of Kabbalah has helped me transform nearly every aspect of my life and showed me a path I couldn't even dream of.

With all I have, I pray that this book creates an even greater certainty in the abundance of the Light in the lives of Ramon and Bickly, and their daughters, Ellia and Ailey and for you and everyone you pray for, too.

There is no greater gift than certainty in the Light.

PREFACE

In this volume of Rav Berg's commentaries on the Torah, dealing with the portions of Miketz, Vayishlach, and Vayechi, we follow the biblical narrative from Joseph's emergence from a dungeon, becoming the second-in-command to Pharaoh; the interpretation of Pharaoh's dreams; the reunion of Joseph with his brothers and father Jacob; and Jacob's blessing of his sons before his death and the passing of Joseph.

The notion of *shichech* (forgetting) is prevalent in these chapters. Here, the Rav expounds on the idea that *shichecha* is an energy-intelligence, a force, that creates a condition of forgetfulness. Not as a result of the absence of memory but rather because a force of darkness called *ketz*, which means "end," causes the memory bank to become covered, creating the illusion that it is seemingly blank.

The Rav's gift as a teacher is the comprehensible manner in which he is able to communicate some of the most mysterious concepts found in religion. Using everyday examples, from the media or common experiences, he unravels the Bible's coded messages with simplicity and humor, clarifying concepts in theoretical physics that even the scientists themselves have trouble explaining.

But, most of all, the following pages are filled with the light and love that lies at the heart of the Rav's relationship with the wisdom of Kabbalah. The Rav's commentaries reveal to the reader practical ways in which kabbalistic principles can be applied to increase the measure of happiness, joy, and peace in life and throughout the world. "This," says the Rav, "is the only purpose of the Bible. Everything else is meaningless."

Here he demonstrates how the Bible achieves this purpose through the meaning and energy found in the text itself. Those who have been put off reading the Bible by the confusion, contradiction, and often sheer nonsense seemingly found in many of its stories, will find an entirely new and thrilling way in which to peruse and understand them, discovering there the real message and gift intended. As the Rav says here: "…we learn both from the Talmud and in the Zohar that the Bible is an instrument with which we can radically improve our lives." Who among us does not ardently wish to accomplish this?

It is not necessary for the reader to review the volumes in a specific order, for they serve solely to attain the above-stated goal; and this objective is achieved and found in abundance wherever we dip into the text. For example, many have wondered why Jacob is sometimes called Israel and sometimes not. Here we discover why this apparent anomaly exists and what it offers to us today.

Referring constantly to the other great sages, as well as to the seminal kabbalistic texts, Rav Berg awakens a curiosity and desire for the wisdom. To learn more and to know more about this eternal wisdom that has never been so widely accessible as it is now through the Kabbalah Centres' work.

The perplexities and conundrums of Kabbalah were for another time. The Rav's great clarification of all the mysteries is for this age—the Age of Aquarius. The unique Three Column System, and the principle of restriction intrinsic to it are now offered to all in the works of Rav Berg, who diligently points to their indispensable utility as weapons in the war to transform life on this planet. Such a transformation will only come to pass through changing oneself from a person only desiring to receive for the self alone into the fully human being with a nature that has a desire and seeks to share all with all. "This," the Rav tells us, "is the way forward out of the mire and up to the mountaintop, where the air is clean and no shadows block the Light."

TABLE OF CONTENTS

BOOK OF BERESHEET:

Portion of Miketz

PORTION OF MIKETZ

Zot Chanukah, the Month of Tevet and Tzadikim

Kabbalah emphasizes the technology that the Torah can provide for us in the ongoing war against Satan, which has been waged now for thousands of years.

The eighth day of Chanukah, called Zot Chanukah, falls on the second day of the month of Tevet (Capricorn), which contains no other holidays. Both the Talmud and the Zohar remark on the importance of Tevet, stating that the energy of Tevet is unequal to all of the other months that contain a holiday. On Zot Chanukah, we have the ultimate energy of the Light and the Vessel—the Vessel of the highest intensity and revelation of the highest Light.

Kabbalah relates this same idea to *tzadikim*, the righteous people. We think of them as having no Desire to Receive, and we believe they abstain from the desires of the world but this is not so. Chariots, like Moses, began at a lower level and elevated, while Joseph emerged to the level of Zeir Anpin. It is interesting that the ascensions of both Moses and Joseph took place in Egypt, thereby making it a very powerful country.

As we read this story, it is important for us to seek out the significance of the metaphors found in these events. And by doing so we are permitted entry into the immaterial, non-observable realm where the five senses have no effect. We are so familiar with this physical world that we can sometimes forget there is another universe beyond it. While he was in Egypt, Joseph emerged from a dungeon and, overnight, became the second-in-command to Pharaoh. Egypt was the country that exercised the most powerful witchcraft and, through it, controlled the universe, yet still no man there could interpret Pharaoh's dreams.

Egypt exemplifies its remarkable energy in two ways: There is the Nile River that flows against gravity—from the South to the North (a river usually flows from North to South)—and there are the Pyramids. No architect or builder even today can duplicate what was built in ancient Egypt.

Beresheet 41:1 When two full years had passed,

Remembering

All occurrences in our universe have been predestined, and scientists now agree that tomorrow can be theoretically known today. However, science has one problem with this idea: Why do we not remember what was yesterday and know what is to be tomorrow? The portion of Miketz addresses this aspect of memory.

At the end of the previous portion of Vayeshev, we read that while he was in jail Joseph interpreted the dreams of Pharaoh's two servants—a baker and a wine steward—who were also incarcerated there with him. In Beresheet 40:14, Joseph told the wine steward: "When all goes well with you, remember me and show me kindness, mention me to Pharaoh and get me out of this prison." What was the good that Joseph did for this wine steward? Why should the wine steward remember him? All that Joseph said was, after all, only his opinion of what the dream meant. Yet both dreams came true, just as Joseph had interpreted them. The Bible then tells us the wine steward was restored to his previous position as Pharaoh's chief cupbearer, and in Beresheet 40:23 we read that he did not remember Joseph.

Rashi (Rav Shlomo Yitzchaki, 1040 – 1105) explains that the wine steward forgot because Joseph depended on the kindness of the wine steward to remember him, instead of praying to God to release him from prison. He placed his trust in a human being—and this is the reason he remained in the dungeon for another two years. The Zohar has a different interpretation, however. In reading the Zohar, we expand our consciousness, and thereby everything we discuss in the Zohar will be understood from a higher level than that to which we are accustomed. The Zohar says:

5

"And it came to pass at the end." HE ASKS, "What is the meaning of 'the end'?" Rav Shimon replied that this is a place in which there is no remembrance—the end of the Left. What does this mean? For it is written, "But think of me (lit. "remember") when it shall be well with you." (Beresheet 40:14) HE ASKS, "Is it proper for Joseph the righteous to say, 'But remember me?'" AND HE ANSWERS, "When Joseph looked at the dream, he said, 'This is assuredly a dream of remembrance,' but he was wrong because it all came from the Holy One, blessed be He. Therefore, the place of forgetfulness rose against him. It is written, 'Nevertheless the chief butler did not remember Joseph, but forgot him.'" HE ASKS, "If it is said 'the chief butler did not remember,' why then add 'but forgot him'?" HE ANSWERS, "'…but forgot him' indicates the place in which there is forgetfulness, which is CALLED the 'end on the side of darkness.'" HE ASKS, "What are the two years?" AND HE ANSWERS, "The grade of forgetfulness returned after that time to the grade in which there is remembrance.

'…that Pharaoh dreamed, and behold, he stood by the river' concerns the dream of Joseph, NAMELY A DREAM OF REMEMBRANCE THAT REFERS TO JOSEPH, because every river is part of Joseph the Righteous. This is the hidden meaning of the thought that whoever sees a river in his dream sees peace, WHICH IS THE GRADE OF YESOD, THAT IS, JOSEPH, as it is written, 'I will extend peace to her like a river,' (Yeshayah 66:12) so 'river' alludes to Joseph."
—Zohar, Miketz 1:7-9

Rav Shimon says that the word *miketz* means "where there is no memory." We have within us consciousness—a force that stores information but does not permit that information to be revealed.

Once we come in contact with certain information, we absorb this information and place it in our mind's computer, yet when we ask for a recall, when we ask to tap into that same consciousness, we find a blank. It is not that there is a malfunction because we are still functioning. Nevertheless, and for whatever reason, we cannot seem to grasp or recall that memory. The Zohar says this means the end of the end, which always means Left Column.

Without Rav Ashlag's very lengthy discourse on just these few words of the Zohar, we could not understand what is taking place in this portion at all. Rav Ashlag explains that the aspect of remembering, or of failing to have a recall of information, depends on one aspect: whether or not we are tapping into the energy of the Central Column—and it is this Central Column that permits the aspect of free will. The Central Column is the energy-intelligence that makes things move, work, and structure themselves in an orderly fashion.

The Zohar says the Hebrew word *zechartani* (remember me) seems to be confusing. *Zechartani* is from the root word *zechor* (remember), and wherever the word *zechor* is mentioned it connotes the word *zachar* (male), which is a connotation of positive energy force. Male is the force of new life; woman is like Mother Earth; she brings the force of the sperm into fruition. However, the force is transmitted via the male. Therefore, because the word *zechor* or *zachar* means an energy force, when we come across a word like *zechartani*, we now know that we are dealing with a positive energy force—and this is a clue that comes from the cosmic code of the Bible.

There is the internal force and there is the body. In our universe, a soul cannot operate without a body—no pure, unadulterated energy force can become revealed unless it first becomes concealed. This is a universal rule. Therefore, for all the hidden knowledge of the universe to be revealed, it must first be concealed—and this same law applies to the Bible itself. This is why the Bible was presented in such a concealed, abstrusely coded form.

As we have discussed before, there can be no flow of energy unless we have the presence of Right, Left, and Central Column. If one of these columns is missing then we cannot access the flow of energy, the potential in our minds, and all the information that we acquired yesterday. We are not capable of accessing this kind of information because the Central Column, which means restriction, is not a constant feature in our human mental computer. It is like shutting off the electrical current in a computer. When we turn off the computer, does this mean that the information has vanished? No. All the information is still there; it has just not been activated.

Therefore, the Zohar tells us that the reason we have a loss of memory, or we cannot access into tomorrow, is because we have not applied restriction. A *tzadik* (righteous person), in this case Joseph, does not exist in the realm of yesterday, today, and tomorrow. He was not concerned with how it will work out in the end or if his position will be maintained. Joseph could see from beginning to end that everything was, is, and always will be good. Once a righteous person reaches this level, he or she knows and is certain that they are already being maintained; and so they do not have to maintain their own position. This is the difference between the righteous person and most of the rest of us. We are always trying to maintain and retain our position, while the righteous person is constantly connected with the total reality because the Central Column makes it so the connection never ceases to exist. It is always operative. Therefore, if someone has a lapse of memory it is because he has lost touch with the Central Column consciousness and falls right back into the Realm of Illusion. The Zohar says if we constantly bring the Central Column into its proper position, then that circuit of energy of today and tomorrow is constant. When we do not access the Central Column, there is a constant battle between the forces of Right and Left, meaning the Desire to Share and the Desire to Receive, whether we are consciously aware of it or not. This explains the ups and downs we all experience. Right and Left are constantly at war with one another. Each cannot get its point across because both make an attempt to block out the other one. Therefore, this aspect of remembering, of maintaining a level of consciousness, does not exist for most people.

What is the secret? When we are in a battle we are so busy with maintaining ourselves that we become consumed in the everyday movement of up and down, and we cannot see the wood for the trees. However, if we inject the energy-intelligence of the Central Column, then there is a balance between the Right and Left, and we have an even, constant flow.

Three Branches that Brought Forth Grapes

The Zohar explains that when the wine steward said there were three branches in his dream that brought forth grapes, Joseph understood that the Three Column System was present. This is why he forecast that Pharaoh would restore the wine steward to his former position. When we try to interpret dreams, more often than not we take into account the insignificant parts of the dream rather than the significant ones. Because a dream is an aspect of prophecy, its message is concealed. For Joseph, the three branches of grapes was the significant part, and from it he knew that the Lightforce was present. There he saw that *zechirah* (remembering the Lightforce) was present—that this force had become revealed. He understood that both aspects of the Shield of David (the Magen David) had become revealed. The Magen David is made up of two triads: the Upper Triad represents the potential, and the Lower Triad is the actual, when things become manifest.

For example, the idea of establishing a school comes to an individual; and then how to establish that school becomes a manifest idea. This all takes place in the Upper Triad—still only in potential. How is this person sure that the idea will become manifest on a potential level? When he questions his motives to make this school, does he want to do it solely for profit or does he want to create a school so he can help others? If he is doing this to benefit himself, and also for the benefit of others, then he establishes and injects the energy of the Central Column in a potential state and then the Upper Triad has become established. He has injected the Third Column energy and completed the circuit of the Upper Triad. If we do not complete this kind of circuit in the Upper Triad, one way or another we are doomed to failure. But this is not all that goes into a building. What follows next is the planning stage. This is still another level, but it has now become more manifest—we are going see something tangible for the first time.

When Joseph heard about the three clusters, he assumed that the Lightforce had become established, meaning it was now time for him to make an exit because he is the Central Column of the Lower Triad. He was able to experience what was happening to him, and at the same time he was observing himself in prison. He was a participant in the movie of his life, and at the same time he was also sitting in the movie theatre watching the movie.

When Rabbi Akiva was brought out by the Romans to be tortured to death, what he actually did, according to the Zohar, was have an out-of-body experience. He did not feel a thing, even to the extent that nothing was really even happening—it was all a complete illusion. The Romans thought they were torturing him but Rabbi Akiva only suffered pain for the first moment because he was prepared to experience the suffering. He injected the Central Column, by saying that it did not bother him if his body had to suffer. If this is what he had to do, for whatever reason, so that the body should be devoid of a Desire to Receive for Oneself Alone, it was all right by him. The only part of him feeling pain would be the body. He accepted it, and the minute he did he had an out-of-body experience—therefore nothing at all really happened to him.

In the same way, when Joseph was thrust into prison, he knew that the body would have to go through this experience but, insofar as he was concerned, he did not experience the illusionary structure in his life. At one moment he is a free man and the most beloved of Jacob's children ("up" in life), and the next minute he is in jail ("down"); a minute later again and he is second-in-command to Pharaoh ("up" again). These are all aspects of the illusionary world. Joseph did not go through these changes because he was on the level of watching himself in the movie; instead he knew the purpose of it all and was not affected by it.

With regard to the dream of the wine steward, Joseph thought that the Lower Triad, where Yesod becomes manifest, was now going to become joined with the Upper Triad, the World of Reality, and that he would be taken out of this illusory jail he was in. Joseph mistakenly assumed that because he was told there were three branches of grape clusters it meant the Lower Triad of the Magen David had become manifest. It is with regard to the realm of the Lower Triad that he made the mistake. The Zohar says Joseph was in no way depending on the wine steward. When he said Joseph should have placed his trust in God, Rashi did not mean that Joseph literally did not place his trust in God, but rather that he should have understood that this dream was still dealing with the Upper Triad and not the Lower Triad. The word for God (Heb. *Kadosh Baruch Hu*) means the Upper Triad. Joseph should have understood that the level of revealment was still in a potential state, and that its time had not yet arrived.

Joseph made the mistake when he said the word *zechartani*, which in this case means "manifestation" and not "remember." But to assume that Joseph, even for a moment, placed his trust in the wine steward has no basis at all, and no meaning. We are dealing here with an individual who is a chariot.

Now why did the wine steward not remember Joseph? When we suddenly forget something that has happened, does it mean that it no longer exists, no longer happened? No. In spirituality anything of a metaphysical nature never disappears. Once something has been recorded on a metaphysical level it is eternal, and information that is registered in the mind is certainly not physical. We can write something down on a piece of paper, and the piece of paper can be destroyed, but the energy contained within the letters we wrote will not be destroyed. We will have no physical access to refer back to the writing on paper, since it no longer exists. But in the mind it never disappears. The proof of this is that, at a later date, we are able suddenly to remember what was written, and thus access the information.

The Zohar explains that there is a force, an energy-intelligence known as *shichecha* (forgetfulness) that creates a condition where we suddenly do not remember. Forgetfulness is not the absence of remembering. Why does the Bible first tell us that the wine steward did not remember Joseph, and follows with "he forgot"? Surely, if we do not remember, this means we forgot. Is it not a repetition of the same idea? The Zohar says that the Bible is revealing the secret of what is the nature of forgetting and what is the nature of remembering—in other words, what is memory and what is a memory lapse. The aspect of forgetting is not that the memory is not working. No. There is a force called *chosheh* (darkness), and it is referred to as *ketz*, which means "end." When the Bible says the wine steward did not remember, it is not discussing remembering in a literal sense of the word, but rather it is discussing the force known by its code name of *ketz*. The energy force of *ketz* causes the bank of memory to become, just for the moment, an illusionary blank. We know this because the Zohar explains that the force of *zechira* (the energy force of "remembering") was not there because a force that is part of the dark forces called *shichecha* (forgetfulness) was present—creating the illusion that "remembering" was not present. This is what happens when we are looking for our car keys all over the house and they have been right there in front of us or in our hand the whole time. At this moment, there is a temporary, illusionary force that can make things disappear.

When a magician makes a 747 Boeing Jet disappear in front of thousands of people, what that magician does not know or does not realize is that he is actually activating the realm of *shichecha*, a force that exists in each and every one of his audience members, so that they see a blank, as if nothing exists there—and this is the force of illusion, a force governed by *ketz* (end). End is finite and is coded in the form of *ketz*. This portion indicates that everything taking place was in the realm of illusion—and this was the mistake that Joseph made. But how could he have made the mistake if he was a chariot?

The answer is that he did not make a mistake. We need to stop ourselves from falling into the trap of thinking that he suffered two extra years because he was disappointed at the wine steward's memory lapse. We have established that Joseph is a chariot and he was not maintaining his own life, but rather his life was maintaining him. Therefore, he was already out of the dungeon, out of the jail before he got into it. In reality, what he was doing was merely watching a movie of the physical Joseph going through these periods of ups and downs. The real Joseph, meaning the one who was watching the movie, knew this whole process was really just a part of the cosmic structure. The Israelites were destined ultimately to go down into Egypt for their *tikkun* (spiritual correction). The Israelites in Egypt were the same Israelites who were in the generation of the Deluge, and they were also the same Israelites who were present at the Tower of Babel incident, yet still had not learned their lesson. Therefore, those same Israelites now had to return again to go through a cleansing period of incarnation in Egypt.

Joseph knew all of this. For him it was all over. He knew that for the illusionary realm there was a purpose, and that this purpose was not for him. The illusion is that Joseph was in Egypt, that there would be worldwide hunger, and that this hunger would bring all of the world's people into Egypt—including the Israelites. Joseph knew from the beginning that the Israelites would become slaves, and go through all that this slavery entailed. What concerned Joseph was the question of whether the part of the movie show that included his incarceration in jail was over with or not. Imagine how thrilling it is to see your movie on the screen and not be affected by it. What a great feeling that must be! We should all try to experience it from time to time.

The wine steward did not remember because there was the aspect of *shichecha* (forgetfulness), the illusion; it was not that he did not want to remember. The scene where the manifestation of Joseph emerging from prison had not arrived yet, and the force of *chashecha* ("darkness," which is same letters as *shichecha* "forgetfulness"), the force that floats around us all day and night, prevented the wine steward from revealing Joseph's dream interpretation to Pharaoh, since this would have meant that Joseph could then emerge from jail. The show must be played out. This, according to the Zohar, is the reason the wine steward did not remember. At times an illusionary force known as *ketz* prevents us from remembering, prevents us from accessing our memory bank.

In Beresheet 41:1, it says, "And it came to pass at the end of two years," but the Hebrew words used are *shenataim yamim* (which literally means "the days of two years"). Where is the translation of the word "days" (Heb. *yamim*)? Why was this word overlooked? There is no reason for the Bible to inject the word *yamim* into the text if it did not have significance. The Zohar extracts another secret from the word *yamim* that we can use in daily life. If during the process of anything we do, both in the realm of the actual (Lower Triad) and or in the realm of the potential (Upper Triad), we constantly inject the force of *zechira*, which means the Central Column, we are assured of a constant connection to the Lightforce. In other words, *yamim* tells us that there has to be the Central Column of the Upper Triad, as well as the Central Column of the Lower Triad.

For example, there are an infinite number of ideas that come to mind regarding the construction of a building—it could be any type of building. Once I localize the thought into what type of building, I have now reduced the idea—and remember, in every reduction there is a price. All ideas are great but not all ideas become great realities because the moment the idea of constructing a building becomes actualized, even just in the mind, I have already placed a limitation on it. When I decide the type of building it is to be—apartment or office et cetera—I am already removing the idea from that all-inclusive realm called "building," and thus I have now limited the original idea of constructing a building. In other words, I have taken it out of the realm of the pure idea of constructing a building, and I have now concentrated on one particular kind of building. The moment my mind has done this, I have reduced the pure idea, with all of its potency, with all of its power, and I have subjected it to a small finite idea. Where this idea could have been infinite, now it is finite. This is neither good nor bad, though, because the idea itself has not changed—that still includes everything. What makes an idea good or bad is whether or not we inject the Central Column energy force into this idea. When Central Column energy is injected into an idea, at this point there is never failure.

With the Central Column energy infused into the idea, I have not contained or reduced the idea but rather I have actually broadened it. It will now become manifested correctly because I have injected into the idea the concept that it is not for me alone. This is the thinking consciousness that must go into every single idea of our life if we want to assure its success, meaning that it is not only worthwhile just in terms of money but also in terms of freedom from aggravation. We are talking now of a total inclusiveness of what is good for us, without limiting it to one aspect or another— this is the totality of beneficence that comes when we connect with the Lightforce.

We learn in Kabbalah that it is easier to operate on the seed than on the tree. This is because we get to it before things become manifest in the wrong way, and this is how we can have all-inclusive beneficence from whatever idea we want to make manifest. Now that all of this has become established in the mind, it will still not produce the building. The next step is to take the vision I have in my mind and make it actual, which involves an architect designing it on paper. Only now are we talking about the actualization. Yet how do we know for certain that it will work out? If it is in the wrong location, it may not be rented. An infinite amount of problems could arise from the decision of placing it in one area or another.

Then comes the second restriction that must be injected, which makes the actual become actual—and this is Yesod. Once again it is about questioning whether the location of this building is going to be just for my benefit or will it benefit others as well? If there is a consciousness of sharing, then another stage of restriction, the one referred to as Yesod, has now been injected into the idea. When these two restrictions, Tiferet of the Upper Triad and Yesod of the Lower Triad, have become manifested, only then is success there because we have insured the removal of any uncertainty, of any illusionary doubts that could arise.

Therefore, according to the Zohar, the Bible is not referring to years. It is telling us that when the two Triads of the Magen David emerge with their Central Columns, Tiferet and Yesod, there is no question that the time for success has come; that the time for Joseph to leave the prison has come because the Lower Triad has been merged with the Upper Triad. But the cosmos had not yet come together to create this situation for Joseph to reveal the purpose of his having been sold into Egypt, to become second-in-command to Pharaoh, and to be the instrument who brings Jacob and all of his family into Egypt.

Joseph knew he would emerge from the prison. However, there was a cosmic timetable determining when this would happen—and this had nothing to do with him or anyone else. If he was doing what he had to do, it was going to happen. We think we are in control, and we think we make our destiny manifest. No. We can only make manifest which path we choose; but once we have chosen a particular program there is almost nothing that the average individual can do to alter that cassette in mid-stream. The only time we can change from one program to another, from a better program to in an even better one, is by virtue of the Magen David, by this process of the two restrictions. Restriction is our only form of free will. The only way to remove ourselves from the Illusionary Reality into an Upper Realm is when these two Sefirot come into play.

The Zohar says that Joseph was depressed until the time they brought him out from the dungeon. What is a depressed state? A depressed state is similar to a depressed car tire, when all of its air has gone out. Someone who has fulfillment has no place within his or her life for depression. When someone is depressed, it means that the Light, the energy that is so vital to keep an individual moving and alive, has become depressed. The Light has not been removed but has been pressed down, and a vacuum—meaning time, space and motion—has been created. How could it be that Joseph had come to a state of depression? We are talking about Joseph, who, in addition to his physical, corporeal level of consciousness, was also a chariot of Yesod. His realm of consciousness was a revealed and open-minded state of reality. Most of us live in the Realm of Illusion for most of the time; we do not connect to the internal 99 Percent Realm, which is the level of Zeir Anpin. When we pray and perform the precepts, it is for no other reason than to connect with the World of Reality, the world where time, space, and motion cease to exist for us. Those who are connected to Zeir Anpin do see tomorrow, do see the next day—just as the prophets did. According to the Zohar, seeing tomorrow and the next day is not only reserved for prophets, it is reserved for anyone who can rise above the 1 Percent Illusionary Reality and connect to the 99 Percent World of Reality.

The depression that overcomes people is actually a result of being moved down into the World of Illusion—and the consequence of being thrust into an Illusory Reality brings depression. But depression is not by and of itself a cause—it is an effect. We bring on this depression by removing ourselves from the true reality. We have to battle each day with the meditations and prayer connections that we have learned through Kabbalah, to keep our heads at least a little above water because below water is the physical Illusionary World, the world where no one sees anything, where we are completely overwhelmed, completely surrounded by what we think are insurmountable conditions.

The Hebrew word for depressed, *atzvut*, comes from the word *etzev*, which means "a nerve." What does the word "depressed" have to with "a nerve"? Someone who is nervous is not necessarily depressed, nor is someone who is depressed necessarily nervous. Depression is the result of an imbalance in the central nervous system. Sometimes, when we watch a movie, we are moved by it and we cry. This is why it is called a "movie"—we are *moved*. But it is only a movie, not our own life, so why do we identify with it? The Zohar explains that when we are affected, it is our life. In other words, we have our life, and yet there is another part of us that is also our life – a part we may not even be aware of. When we get emotional, we are identifying with another aspect of ourselves, which is not within our reality, yet it is still a reality—we are either still there now, or else we were there during a particular situation.

When Joseph saw himself still in prison, he realized that the cosmic structure of the two Triads had not yet become a reality, and so he was depressed. Just for a moment, he had identified with this scene. Joseph saw that the time had not yet come. Time was being stretched out. Things were moving in slow motion, and it bothered him. He was concerned because the Central Column still had not come into place.

Miketz and End

The second word of the first verse of this portion is *miketz*, which means "end." Rashi explains that because *acharei miketz* means "after the end," it indicates there are many difficulties in the few verses under discussion.

The portion of Miketz begins by telling us that after a period of ten years Joseph was punished because he depended upon the wine steward to remember his power of dream interpretation and, therefore, had to suffer another two years in prison.

While in that dungeon, however, Joseph was in total control. Wherever he was, under whatever conditions he faced, Joseph was always the cause and in control of every situation—thus it is that Joseph can give us insight into our own behavior. Learning at the Kabbalah Centres has also given us an opportunity to begin taking control over our lives. What the Bible is telling us, is that the reason problems do not end is because of our tendency to surrender our minds to the Satan. Satan does not necessarily exist to incite us to commit crimes and violations. Satan's purpose, as it has been for thousands of years, is to make certain that humankind does not have control over our own consciousness. And he accomplishes this merely by feeding our ego.

We are under the misconception that we have control. This is Satan's major weapon. The simple rule is that the moment we are aware we lack control, this is when we come to understand we are in a war against the Satan's coercion. His job is to convince us to relinquish control over our minds.

Try to take one minute to quiet the mind. Why is this so difficult? Lock yourself in a room where no one can disturb you and, after a mere sixty seconds, how many of us can say we did not have a single thought? Thousands of thoughts cross our minds in one moment. We do not have control over them. The ego is so strong. We can see examples of this everywhere, especially among the most successful people. To what do we attribute our success? Do we not attribute it to our own abilities, to everything about ourselves? What we learn from Joseph is that he represents Yesod; he maintained a level of awareness in the Flawless Universe; he maintained an awareness that there is another place, not in Heaven but in his own consciousness, a place where he could maintain control.

This is what the Kabbalah Centres are about, waging a war against the Satan. The Satan can convince us that we are in control when we are not—and he succeeds more often than he does not.

Joseph was always in charge while he was in the dungeon, and wherever else he was too, because he knew that this is a constant struggle. Whether we are in a prison, a strange house or wherever we are, there will always be a constant struggle. We must never lose sight of this fact, and realize that it is an incessant battle and, therefore, strive to maintain our consciousness. Then, and only then, will we find there is nothing in this world that we cannot overcome—nothing that is of a physical nature. When I say nothing, I am not speaking about the nonsensical things; I am talking about serious matters. We have to accept the idea that we are not in control, and that we are engaged in a battle to regain control, that there is a war being waged every moment of every day. We can overcome the idea that we are in control! There are many tests that science has devised to determine the capacity of the brain, and these tests show that we are not in control of our minds. Science says our minds are 99 percent of who we are, and not the one percent physicality in which we usually place most of the emphasis.

Joseph and Miketz

Vayehi miketz refers to Joseph. From the story, it appears that Joseph went from one prison to another. In the same way that many people are moved from one location to another, Joseph's address merely changed to that of another prison. But this time it says "at the end of two years." The word *miketz* means "the end," and the Zohar says this was the end of the *galut* (exile) of that period.

Many of us feel that we have been in exile for 2,000 years and that it is more than we can bear. Yet it serves us to know that the Israelites were in exile for longer than 200 years.

The Zohar quotes *Vayehi miketz shenatayim yamin*, translating it as: *Vayehi* (and it came to be); *miketz* (at the end) *shenatayim* (two years) *yamin* (days). First it says two years, and then it says days. The Zohar, like all the other commentators asks, which is it—years or days? First the Bible says years and then it says days. Although the Zohar itself is in concealment, there is so much more information within its text. So what this sentence means is that for Joseph, the years seemed like days. But for us, because of the challenges we face, the days can often seem like years.

The Zohar does not permit us to think, even for a moment, that Joseph the Righteous was an ordinary criminal. Rav Shimon has a completely different understanding of Joseph—that he represents a higher dimension. Joseph is Yesod, which is one level higher than Malchut—but it is not a question of level and scale. It does not work that way. The level of Yesod is far beyond Malchut, so much higher in fact that Joseph literally governs Malchut. He is the master of sharing all that exists in the world of Malchut. It all comes down through the Sefira Yesod, which is known as the Sefira of Joseph the Righteous. With this understanding, the portion of Miketz can be easily grasped—so let us put this into our frame of consciousness.

Pharaoh had a dream: He was standing by the Nile, 2 when out of the river there came up seven cows, sleek and fat, and they grazed among the reeds. 3 After them seven other cows, ugly and gaunt, came up out of the Nile and stood beside those on the riverbank. 4 And the cows that were ugly and gaunt ate up the seven sleek, fat cows. Then Pharaoh woke up. 5 He fell asleep again and had a second dream: Seven heads of grain, healthy and good, were growing on a single stalk. 6 After them, seven other heads of grain sprouted— thin and scorched by the east wind. 7 The thin heads of grain swallowed up the seven healthy, full heads. Then Pharaoh woke up; it had been a dream. 8 In the morning his mind was troubled, so he sent for all the magicians and wise men of Egypt. Pharaoh told them his dreams, but no one could interpret them for him. 9 Then the chief cupbearer said to Pharaoh, "Today I am reminded of my faults. 10 Pharaoh was once angry with his servants, and he imprisoned me and the chief baker in the house of the captain of the guard. 11 Each of us had a dream the same night, and each dream had a meaning of its own. 12 Now a young Hebrew was there with us, a servant of the captain of the guard. We told him our dreams, and he interpreted them for us, giving each man the interpretation of his dream. 13 And things turned out exactly as he interpreted them to us: I was restored to my position, and the other man was hanged." 14 So Pharaoh sent for Joseph, and he was quickly brought from the dungeon. When he had shaved and changed his clothes, he came before Pharaoh. 15 Pharaoh said to Joseph, "I had a dream, and no one can interpret it. But I have heard it said of you that when you hear a dream you can interpret it." 16 "I cannot do it," Joseph replied to Pharaoh, "but God will give Pharaoh the answer he desires." 17 Then Pharaoh said to Joseph, "In my dream I was standing on the bank of the Nile, 18 when out of the river there came up seven cows, fat and sleek, and they grazed among the reeds. 19 After them, seven other cows came up—scrawny and very ugly and lean. I had never seen such ugly cows in all the land of Egypt. 20 The lean, ugly cows ate up the seven fat cows that came up first. 21 But even after they ate them, no one could tell that they had done so; they looked just as ugly as before. Then I woke up. 22 In my dreams I also saw seven heads of grain, full and good, growing on a single stalk. 23 After them, seven other heads sprouted—withered and thin and scorched by the east wind. 24 The thin heads of grain swallowed up the seven good heads. I told this to the magicians, but none could explain it to me." 25 Then Joseph said to Pharaoh, "The dreams of Pharaoh are one and the same. God has revealed to Pharaoh what He is about to do. 26 The seven good cows are seven years, and the seven good heads of grain are seven years; it is one and the same dream. 27 The seven lean, ugly cows that came up afterward are seven

years, and so are the seven worthless heads
of grain scorched by the east wind: They are
seven years of famine. 28 It is just as I said to
Pharaoh: God has shown Pharaoh what He
is about to do. 29 Seven years of great abundance are coming throughout the land of
Egypt, 30 but seven years of famine will follow them. Then all the abundance in Egypt
will be forgotten, and the famine will ravage
the land. 31 The abundance in the land will
not be remembered because the famine that
follows it will be so severe. 32 The reason the
dream was given to Pharaoh in two forms
is that the matter has been firmly decided
by God, and God will do it soon. 33 And now
let Pharaoh look for a discerning and wise
man and put him in charge of the land of
Egypt. 34 Let Pharaoh appoint commission-
ers over the land to take a fifth of the har-
vest of Egypt during the seven years of abundance. 35 They should collect all the food of
these good years that are coming and store
up the grain under the authority of Pharaoh,
to be kept in the cities for food. 36 This food
should be held in reserve for the country, to
be used during the seven years of famine
that will come upon Egypt, so that the country may not be ruined by the famine." 37 The
plan seemed good to Pharaoh and to all his
officials. 38 So Pharaoh asked them, "Can
we find anyone like this man, one in whom is
the spirit of God?" 39 Then Pharaoh said to
Joseph, "Since God has made all this known
to you, there is no one so discerning and wise

as you. **40 You shall be in charge of my palace, and all my people are to submit to your orders. Only with respect to the throne will I be greater than you." 41 So Pharaoh said to Joseph, "I hereby put you in charge of the whole land of Egypt." 42 Then Pharaoh took his signet ring from his finger and put it on Joseph's finger. He dressed him in robes of fine linen and put a gold chain around his neck. 43 He had him ride in a chariot as his second-in-command, and men shouted before him, "Make way!" Thus he put him in charge of the whole land of Egypt. 44 Then Pharaoh said to Joseph, "I am Pharaoh, but without your word no one will lift hand or foot in all Egypt." 45 Pharaoh gave Joseph the name Zaphenath-Paneah and gave him Asenath, daughter of Potiphera, priest of On, to be his wife. And Joseph went throughout the land of Egypt.**

The Dreams of Pharaoh

The portion of Miketz is about two dreams that Pharaoh dreamt. One dream was about seven cows that were well fed and looked substantial, and seven other cows that looked starved with no meat on their bones. The starved cows devoured the fat ones, and at this point Pharaoh awoke. He then had a second dream about stalks of grain in the fields, and this dream shared the same theme: the seven healthy stalks were devoured by seven unhealthy stalks.

The Zohar and Rashi ask where these cows came from. The Bible is very specific here about telling us that Pharaoh was standing by the

Nile River when he saw these cows emerge from the water. Why is it so important for us to know where the cows came from? A dream is a dream. Why does the Bible have to tell us he was standing by the Nile, from which the cows came out?

No one in Pharaoh's court understood the meaning of this dream. Pharaoh asked all his wise men, and none could provide an answer. Then the wine steward remembered Joseph's interpretation of his dream two years earlier, and that everything Joseph said came true. So Joseph was brought out of the dungeon to interpret Pharaoh's dreams.

Pharaoh recounted his dream to Joseph differently from the way it is first described in the Bible. The Bible states that the diseased cows devoured the healthy cows, and that then Pharaoh woke up. When Pharaoh recounted the dream to Joseph, however, he said that the diseased cows ate the seven healthy cows, and then he added that there was no change in them—they remained diseased, and then he woke up. One would think because they had just devoured the healthy cows they would be changed, they would look and feel better but they remained as they were. After Pharaoh told Joseph the second dream, Joseph explained that the seven healthy cows refer to seven years of plenty, after which will come seven years of famine. In hearing this, Pharaoh concluded that Joseph was the wisest man in the world, and so he made Joseph his second-in-command.

What does the Bible want to teach us here? The Bible is completely concealed but it is through this concealment, and by virtue of the Zohar, that we can learn some of the secrets of the universe. This is the purpose of the revelation on Mount Sinai—to reveal the Bible, which is completely mystical. As the Zohar explains, there is not one story in the Bible that can reveal its true intent. The Zohar was provided to the world at the same time as the revelation of the Torah on Mount Sinai. Only because of the Zohar do we understand the secrets that can be revealed from the Bible. Thus it is that the revelation at Mount Sinai is the secret of the universe.

What is revealed here in this story? The Zohar provides a lengthy discussion about Pharaoh's dreams, explaining that because we fail to understand the way the universe operates we fail in life. This is the reason why Pharaoh relates his dream differently and fails to mention that when they were swallowed up it had no effect. The Bible does not state that the diseased cows did not look any better because the Bible is simply relating the facts of Pharaoh's dream. The Bible records what he dreamed and what he told Joseph.

Joseph saw in Pharaoh's dream that what was swallowed up was related to humanity's persistent habit of forgetting life's abundance. Joseph was consequently chosen to be second-in-command to Pharaoh. It may seem that this is a sensible interpretation, but one must question the assumption that out of all of Egypt no one else but Joseph could come to the same conclusion.

Essentially the Bible, a very spiritual compendium of laws, states that the only one who could furnish the interpretation of these dreams was Joseph. This is why we see the story as more than a mere sequence of events. The Zohar explains that what the dream indicates to Joseph is that in seven years, humankind's current consciousness would swallow up the idea that there was ever food anywhere in all the world. The Zohar correlates this to a person who, until the age of 13 for a male and 12 for a female, has nothing else governing their consciousness but Satan. It is only after the age of 12 and 13, respectively for girls and boys that the good inclination of an individual emerges—this being the inclination that extends from God's beneficence. A sharing nature does not exist naturally in a child. In our Kabbalah schools, children are taught about sharing. They are also taught that it is not their given nature to behave in this manner.

From this story we learn that Satan also understood chaos can only be recognized by one who has experienced abundance; and then only upon deprivation of beneficence does one experience lack.

Lack is not the same thing as never having tasted goodness or abundance. It is like someone who has only experienced living in a hut, someone who never knew that people could also live in mansions. Such a person cannot experience deprivation because they have not yet tasted the other condition of life. Lack within individuals might arise out of envy when they see there is another world out there containing things they do not have themselves. What we learn here is that to inflict the idea of chaos Satan must first provide abundance, otherwise there is no true experience of deprivation. It is only after losing something that we can appreciate what we had.

How does the experience of loss affect an individual? If a person has experienced abundance, and then undergoes deprivation, it is more difficult to understand that the abundance was not self-created. A person is born into good health, and then at some point they lose it. Now that the good health is gone, they may be conscious that all they once had was through the Grace of God. But where was an awareness of the Grace of God when they were enjoying the abundance? The reason Satan is so successful is because the whole idea of Creation and becoming the Creator (as we have studied in Kabbalah) is something unfamiliar to humankind. People near death have been given suggestions about using the Ana Beko'ach prayer and various Names of God, we see this all the time, and they reject it, they reject using what could create the abundance again. How can this be explained?

It is hard for people to accept that what they lost was not their own creation to begin with. As long as we maintain that our abundance is of our own doing, we will have a difficult time indeed. We will come to a time, like when we connect with this reading, that is so powerful and not take advantage of it. Only because it is so simple. Here we have nothing to do but to tap into the Lightforce of God. We must become aware that each and every single moment we exist is only by the Grace of God. It is His Lightforce that is instilled in us, and it is the stream of this Lightforce that enables our body to function. Science tells us that nature is responsible for our existence; and scientists do not define nature as God.

How long was it before the Egyptians realized they would head into a famine? Even the process of understanding cannot begin without the Lightforce of God. Only with a consciousness that we have the Lightforce of God in us can we achieve a mastery over nature—so we cannot forget from whence the Light in us originated. When ideas arise and we assume they come from us, it is a problem; for then there is an absence of the acknowledgement of God. Without the Lightforce of God, all of this is irrelevant. We need to acknowledge that we are not simply a part of the Lightforce of God but that we are infused with it. We need to place a greater emphasis, not on the physical Torah Scroll but rather on its concealed meaning—the concealed wisdom—concepts that we cannot grasp with the five senses.

Joseph's interpretation of Pharaoh's dreams stress the importance of putting aside food from the seven fat years for the famine to come. And for this wisdom, Joseph became second-in-command to Pharaoh. Pharaoh then divided his kingdom with Joseph on the premise of this dream interpretation. But the story is totally illogical. What is really going on here is that Joseph had achieved the level of Yesod, meaning he elevated himself out of the realm of Malchut—beyond the realm where chaos, pain, and suffering exist. No matter how slight his contribution to Pharaoh might seem to us, this was his destiny. Pharaoh placed Joseph in charge of the physical dimension out of a need for the world to continue on with sustenance. When Joseph achieved the elevated consciousness known as Yesod, he took himself entirely into the realm of the Flawless Universe.

Disease and True Health

What was the reason for two dreams, when both seem so similar? The commentators ask this same question. One dream is about the animal kingdom, and the other about the vegetable kingdom. And what is the purpose of this seemingly insignificant story, in which Joseph becomes second-in-command, almost as powerful as Pharaoh himself?

As we have seen throughout the Bible, there is a recurring theme of water and wells here. When Abraham's servant, Eliezer, traveled to find a wife for Isaac, he met Rebecca by a well. When Jacob fled his home, he also met Rachel by a well. When Moses fled Egypt, it was by a well that he met Tziporah, his future wife. Wells come up all the time because the Bible is teaching us that water is the essence of life. The whole world consists of water; it is 80 to 90 percent water. A human being is also largely made up of water.

We have discussed the essence of water many times. There is also a discussion about a shortage of fruits and vegetables in the world today, which is one reason why food is being modified genetically. However, while a fruit may seem to grow faster now, with genetic manipulation, an apple is no longer really an apple—it is a modified apple. Everything within the modified apple is changed. I do not know why this is being done when food is abundant.

Recent nuclear reactor accidents have spread radiation everywhere. I have been saying for years now that the reason why incidents of cancer and other diseases have increased is because our air, water, and food are contaminated. Everything is contaminated. The media confirm this, yet they also claim that contamination is kept at safe levels. When we are told we can continue to consume something safely, who decides what safe levels of contamination are?

What we draw from this story is that disease is all around us, devouring us, and yet nothing changes, everything remains the same because, although the diseases we are dealing with are detectable, there is no technology to see what is really transpiring here. The diseases that devour us do not turn into better bacteria, ones that are safe or even beneficial for us. We are living in a time that, because of our consciousness and the game Satan plays with us, we do not see the whole picture. When we are well, we think everything is fine. Yet if we looked at the reports on the Chernobyl nuclear disaster, we would realize that every single day, millions of tons of radiation are spreading all around the world. Why do I have to mention it? It is devouring things we do not see and have no idea about, unless we pursue the subject. But most of us are not interested in pursuing what is really happening in the whole world. The contamination is in what we eat and what we drink—it is this serious. The most potent tool to combat all this is the reading of this biblical portion because the Lightforce of God comes through it. There is no other way we can inject the Lightforce into our system to combat what is going on today.

We do not take this seriously because we may not see people falling down dead in the streets—Satan would not permit something so obvious. Therefore, I say we must raise our consciousness. Awareness is the only way we can improve our lives. If we continue on without knowing what is going on around us, within a short space of time we will be facing doom. This may sound terrible but my intention here is not to frighten anyone because we have the tools to counteract such a dire outcome.

The Bible itself is always referred to as water. I have close friends who sometimes miss the reading of Torah on Shabbat, and when they do they apologize to me. Why apologize to *me*? It is like the bank president who says the safe is open from nine to ten in the morning—take all the money you want. But when I cannot make it, I call the bank president and say, "I'm really sorry I couldn't get there."

We do not have reality in our consciousness. Am I trying to promote study of the Bible? Yes, because I do not know any other answer available to us. Extensive studies, have been done and we have seen it with our own eyes; it is so serious. I am not stressing the doom, but rather I am saying we had better begin doing something about the global situation soon. The best path we can take is to insert the Light and remove the darkness. The more Light there is, the darkness, whatever it consists of, will just disappear. This is what the Kabbalah Centres are all about teaching: the way by which we can all reveal more Light.

Joseph and Control

In every predicament he faced Joseph was in control. Even while he was in the dungeon, the jailers gave him full control. Although what he experienced was very uncomfortable, he never lost control. What this portion is helping us understand is that we should be in control even when all around us seems so chaotic. We learn here that even when all appears to be lost, we need to maintain a certainty that this trouble is all a process of cleansing. This does not mean we are in control, however, it does mean we should be happy we are going through this apparent difficulty. When we experience a difficulty, this is when Satan seizes us, so he can confuse us about what is really beneficial for us. This is what Rav Shimon tells us is the answer. One may seek an answer in the new movements but there are 4,000 years behind this idea.

The only time we can experience control is when things are not going well, when it looks like we are not going to make it. In a dungeon, Joseph needed to experience what he went through so he could overcome it. "Three days more," or "three months," this is the verdict some hear, yet so-called terminally ill people still survive—it all depends on consciousness. Thus we can benefit from reflecting on the story of Joseph. He experienced power and control all the time, irrespective of the conditions he faced.

46 Joseph was thirty years old when he entered the service of Pharaoh, king of Egypt. And Joseph went out from Pharaoh's presence and traveled throughout Egypt. 47 During the seven years of abundance the land produced plentifully. 48 Joseph collected all the food produced in those seven years of abundance in Egypt and stored it in the cities. In each city he put the food grown in the fields surrounding it. 49 Joseph stored up huge quantities of grain, like the sand of the sea; it was so much that he stopped keeping records because it was beyond measure. 50 Before the years of famine came, two sons were born to Joseph by Asenath, daughter of Potiphera, priest of On. 51 Joseph named his firstborn Manasseh and said, "It is because God has made me forget all my trouble and all my father's household." 52 The second son he named Ephraim and said, "It is because God has made me fruitful in the land of my suffering." 53 The seven years of abundance in Egypt came to an end, 54 and the seven years of famine began, just as Joseph had said. There was famine in all the other lands, but in the whole land of Egypt there was food. 55 When all Egypt began to feel the famine, the people cried to Pharaoh for food. Then Pharaoh told all the Egyptians, "Go to Joseph and do what he tells you." 56 When the famine had spread over the whole country, Joseph opened the storehouses and sold grain to the Egyptians, for the famine was severe throughout Egypt. 57 And all the

countries came to Egypt to buy grain from Joseph, because the famine was severe in all the world.

Beresheet 42:1 When Jacob learned that there was grain in Egypt, he said to his sons, "Why do you just keep looking at each other?" 2 He continued, "I have heard that there is grain in Egypt. Go down there and buy some for us, so that we may live and not die." 3 Then ten of Joseph's brothers went down to buy grain from Egypt. 4 But Jacob did not send Benjamin, Joseph's brother, with the others, because he was afraid that harm might come to him. 5 So Israel's sons were among those who went to buy grain, for the famine was in the land of Canaan also. 6 Now Joseph was the governor of the land, the one who sold grain to all its people. So when Joseph's brothers arrived, they bowed down to him with their faces to the ground. 7 As soon as Joseph saw his brothers, he recognized them, but he pretended to be a stranger and spoke harshly to them. "Where do you come from?" he asked. "From the land of Canaan," they replied, "to buy food." 8 Although Joseph recognized his brothers, they did not recognize him. 9 Then he remembered his dreams about them and said to them, "You are spies! You have come to see where our land is unprotected." 10 "No, my lord," they answered. "Your servants have come to buy food. 11 We are all the sons of one man. Your servants are honest men, not spies." 12 "No!" he said to them. "You have come to see where our land is unprotected." 13 But they replied, "Your servants were twelve brothers, the sons of one man, who lives in the land of Canaan. The youngest is now with our father, and one is no more." 14 Joseph said to them, "It is just as I told you: You are spies! 15 And this is how you will be tested: As surely as Pharaoh lives you will not leave this place unless your youngest brother comes here. 16 Send one of your number to get your brother; the rest of you will be kept in prison, so that your words may be tested to see if you are telling the truth. If you are not, then as surely as Pharaoh lives you are spies!" 17 And he put them all in custody for three days. 18 On the third day, Joseph said to them, "Do this and you will live, for I fear God: 19 If you are honest men, let one of your brothers stay here in prison, while the rest of you go and take grain back for your starving households. 20 But you must bring your youngest brother to me, so that your words may be verified and that you may not die." This they proceeded to do.

The Nature of the Good Things

Why did Joseph, who was now in control of Egypt and also elevated into the realm of Yesod, not immediately tell his suffering father that he was alive? Nine years after Joseph's disappearance, we hear about his brothers, including Benjamin, whom Jacob would not let out of his sight. How do we reconcile the fact that Joseph, a *tzadik*, did not inform his father that he was alive? (Though of course, Jacob did know on one level). We are discussing chariots here, twelve people who provide us with the opportunity to control the negative influences each of us is inflicted with. The Zohar says we may think that we are the creators of what we have, and that no one can take it away. However, if we are not able to change this way of thinking, this kind of consciousness, we will remain victims. Why should we suffer? Is it God's intention? No one inflicts pain on us but ourselves. Each tribe gives us an opportunity, in each lifetime, to tap into the energy that will enable us to overcome and change our consciousness.

We, too, can act in the same way towards those around us. There are times when we have neglected the fact that we can behave like Joseph. This story applies to those who have always looked upon what they have as something they created themselves. While it is through the effort of our sharing and caring, the abundance we experience does not belong to us, it is there by the Grace of God. We are given here the opportunity to connect directly to the Lightforce of God. We do not feel what we have can be taken away tomorrow. If we do not feel the possibility of lack, that every day is our last chance for connection, we have not made the connection.

Satan has been with us for a very long time; his methods are very successful. There were seven years where the Egyptians and the world enjoyed sustenance, but ultimately it seems to come to an end. No matter what it is, if we think it is our possession, it eventually comes to an end. In this way we never get to experience that we can have permanent control over our lives. Being deprived of health or abundance is a consequence of not paying attention when we have these gifts. What we do not understand is that if we created this good health and abundance in the first place, why can we not retrieve what we lost? Why can we not make the same connection ourselves and make our good re-appear? Science is always finding new ways to keep us healthy and increase longevity, and it continually recommends ways to remedy and prevent disease, when all along it is God's Grace that creates such things as stem cells, health and abundance—all of those things that are not ours to begin with. On Shabbat, we are offered undiluted energy without obstruction, we are offered profound Light to make changes in the memory of our consciousness. In Kabbalah we hear about the mistakes of righteous people and what they were able to do, and we ourselves can also be the participants, the creators, drawing upon the level of this energy that is available when everything is complete and our vessel is at its maximum capacity.

21 They said to one another, "Surely we are being punished because of our brother. We saw how distressed he was when he pleaded with us for his life, but we would not listen; that's why this distress has come upon us." 22 Reuben replied, "Didn't I tell you not to sin against the boy? But you wouldn't listen! Now we must give an accounting for his blood." 23 They did not realize that Joseph could understand them, since he was using an interpreter. 24 He turned away from them and began to weep, but then turned back and spoke to them again. He had Simeon taken from them and bound before their eyes. 25 Joseph gave orders to fill their bags with grain, to put each man's silver back in his sack, and to give them provisions for their journey. After this was done for them, 26 they loaded their grain on their donkeys and left. 27 At the place where they stopped for the night, one of them opened his sack to get feed for his donkey, and he saw his silver in the mouth of his sack. 28 "My silver has been returned," he said to his brothers. "Here it is in my sack." Their hearts sank and they turned to each other trembling and said, "What is this that God has done to us?"

Connecting to the Big Picture

In this section, we want to connect to the bigger picture, to realize everything that happens in our life is part of a bigger picture, helping to cleanse many moments of negativity that we ourselves have injected into it. It is about moving beyond the moment to the bigger picture.

29 When they came to their father Jacob in the land of Canaan, they told him all that had happened to them. They said, 30 "The man who is lord over the land spoke harshly to us and treated us as though we were spying on the land. 31 But we said to him, 'We are honest men; we are not spies. 32 We were twelve brothers, sons of one father. One is no more, and the youngest is now with our father in Canaan.' 33 Then the man who is lord over the land said to us, 'This is how I will know whether you are honest men: Leave one of your brothers here with me, and take food for your starving households and go. 34 But bring your youngest brother to me so I will know that you are not spies but honest men. Then I will give your brother back to you, and you can trade in the land.' " 35 As they were emptying their sacks, there in each man's sack was his pouch of silver! When they and their father saw the money pouches, they were frightened. 36 Their father Jacob said to them, "You have deprived me of my children. Joseph is no more and Simeon is no more, and now you want to take Benjamin. Everything is against me!" 37 Then Reuben said to his father, "You may put both of my sons to death if I do not bring him back to you. Entrust him to my care, and I will bring him back." 38 But Jacob said, "My son will not go down there with you; his brother is dead and he is the only one left. If harm comes to him on the journey you are taking, you will bring my gray head down to the grave in sorrow."

Jacob's Reunion with His Brothers

In the second half of this portion, seven years have passed and there is a famine. Jacob and his sons, living in Israel are told there is food in Egypt, and then the whole story unfolds. Joseph notices his brothers' arrival when they come to buy food, and he plays a game with them. These events seem ridiculous. Why is Joseph doing this? This whole section is about a game he plays with them—and many would accuse him of cruelty. Now that he is second-in-command of Egypt, why does he not let his father know, after seventeen long years, that he is alive? Rather than this, Joseph pursues another course.

This game that Joseph continues to play with his brothers is not only in this section but also in the next portion of Vayigash. Joseph tells them to bring their little brother Benjamin. This is Joseph the Righteous, the *tzadik*. It makes no sense. Rather than follow the events of the story, we should ask ourselves what Joseph wanted or, more importantly, what do we want?

The reason we read this section is because these same games, the ones that Joseph played with his brothers, we play not only with ourselves but with other people, every day. We are not sensitive, just as Joseph was not sensitive to his father or to his brothers. It is true they did something wrong but for how long can one hold a grudge—seventeen years?

What the Bible wants to teach us, which is an idea we have learned before because we continually repeat it in our prayers, is that we want to be with Joseph. This is our connection. We do not ever want to forget it. Throughout our prayers, what is the reason we want to be with Joseph? Is it so he will be our intermediary? We have learned in Kabbalah that there is no intermediary; each person has to bring his or her own blessing. We must remember the three words in the Bible that are said at the splitting of the Red Sea, *ma titzak elai*, meaning "why are you praying to me?" God told the Israelites they could do it themselves. This concept still does not penetrate our consciousness. Joseph is not our intermediary—there is no such thing. We are tapping into the Light that Joseph can provide. We have the tools to tap into the Light—and there is no other answer. The Kabbalah Centres provide the tools to connect with the Light, and nothing more. Infusion is the only answer.

The Question of Joseph's Insensitivity

We cannot play games of insensitivity or intolerance. Before I studied Kabbalah, I never asked the question, why? Why was Joseph doing this? Even Rashi does not raise this question. Instead, Rashi asks how Jacob did not know that Joseph was alive. Jacob had access to a realm where there is no time, no space, and no motion. Rashi's answer is that Jacob lost his *Ruach haKodesh*, his Divine Inspiration. It left him because he was depressed. This is the answer that I accepted in the old days. But we are talking about Jacob here. Was he depressed one day, and then when he meets Joseph he becomes uplifted?

Jacob is showing us that when we enter into a depression or when we enter into the games that are described here, these games that we play prevent the Light funneled through Joseph from reaching us. As we have discussed previously, our own behavior is our enemy. Our behavior towards our fellow human beings, which is the way Joseph behaved with his brothers, and the manner they behaved towards him, this is the enemy.

We do not recognize the Light in other people, especially if we do not know them. A man was walking down the street in a hurry, and someone asked him the time. He said "I'm sorry I can't tell you, I'm in a rush." He was thinking, "Why should I help you of all people?" Then the man who was in a rush looked for his watch and realized he left it at home. So he asked someone else what the time was but the man he asked stuttered, and he had to be patient for the answer. Human dignity toward others can never be replaced. We have it at our disposal—there is nothing missing today. We are in that period of immortality; we are in that period of being able to heal ourselves. So what is wrong? We are playing games, and we cannot play games. We must treat every other person with human dignity, and then everything opens up.

How do we get this strength, this foresight, and this consciousness? We come to Shabbat to listen to the reading of the Bible to remove the games. The Light removes the games and the insensitivities that are within each of us.

Why Bad Things Happen To Good People

We have here the story of the famine that took place all around the world, including Egypt. Not having food, Jacob sends his ten sons down to purchase food in Egypt. And they find their way into the home of Joseph. The Bible says that at this point Joseph remembered an earlier dream in which his brothers bowed down to him. The Zohar asks if Joseph was seeking revenge. Considering that his brothers sold him into slavery, this would be understandable. Thus it seems that Joseph's intent was to put them through the agony of bringing their younger brother, Benjamin, and consequently Jacob to Egypt.

The obvious question that comes to mind here is why his father, Jacob, was responsible. After all, Joseph was alive, and he had seemingly not thought of his father in seventeen years. Thus the Bible tells us Joseph recalled the dream about his brothers bowing down to him, and he realized it was coming true. Yet he did not think for a moment his father may have been filled with pain throughout this period, and that he ought to, at this point, reveal himself to his brothers. Why did he delay the revelation that he was alive, making his father suffer longer?

From what the Bible says, it appears as if this entire scenario was a form of revenge. Yet how can we begin to believe that Joseph the Righteous would behave in such a fashion? We must remember that these people are Chariots, people who had achieved an elevated level of consciousness and are connected to the immaterial world, the universe that knows nothing of time, space, or motion, and where no chaos exists. How can this exist within them?

The Bible is teaching us that these Chariots have the presence of two universes within them. The Zohar and Rav Isaac Luria (the Ari, 1534 – 1572) say that they conduct themselves in such a manner only to teach us that there are two universes. One is known as the Flawless Universe or the Tree of Life Reality where time, space, and motion are not limiting factors, and the other is our world, the world of the Tree of Knowledge, which we are all familiar with, having the limitations of time, space, and motion, where chaos rules.

On this level of the material world there still should be some compensation for the fact that we are told never to bear a grudge, never to seek revenge. If someone has done us wrong, we are to consider that which affected us as part of our own *tikkun* (spiritual correction). Whatever happens to us in this physical world, which is totally governed by the Lightforce, is exclusively a question of cause and effect. The quantum theory says that in this world everything of a physical nature can be changed because it is the lesser world, the one percent of reality, which in fact some consider to be an illusion, and yet there are quite a number of people here who are caught up in this illusion.

This is what the Bible wants to teach us, and if we have not learned this lesson we have not acquired the energy and knowledge of this story. In all of our actions, people who are generally kind and good are not evil. There are of course serial killers and thieves who enjoy what they do, but these are the extremes, the exceptions to the rule, and their only reason is self-satisfaction. These people and the things they do give us cause and reason to believe that this world is random. This is the dilemma: Is there control or is everything random?

Once we have begun to study the rules and principles of Kabbalah, we come to understand that nothing is random. Even the code numbers that banks use are not random. No matter what kinds of codes are created, we have a certain code or discipline so it will conform to some of the ideas that are imbedded in our consciousness. There is nothing random.

Some have trouble believing that a sniper killing victims he never comes in contact with is not random. David Arnold wrote a book, Why Do Bad Things Happen to Good People? This is a valid question, to which the author never gives an answer. Sometimes this world does not seem logical. We forget this because we are limited in the frame of reference of time, space and motion, and we cannot see beyond physicality.

Seeing beyond the illusion is what we hope to achieve. We do not have a complete picture of what is actually transpiring. Prior lifetimes are always separated by time. Once we have achieved access into the world of the Tree of Life, which is the ultimate purpose of all our study, then we begin to realize that no parts to a picture are fragmented, that everything that goes beyond time, space, and motion is what has to be considered.

The Zohar asks, when Joseph remembered his dream, was he thinking about revenge? What the Bible is teaching us is to gain an insight into the world of metaphysics, the spiritual world, the world that does not know of chaos. To move into that realm, one must begin to recognize and know there is no such thing as chaos that cannot be overturned or corrected. We can control the chaos around us.

Our world is called the Illusionary World for this reason: it is here today, gone tomorrow. Below is a picture of a goblet with two profiles that sometimes appears as a goblet and sometimes as two profiles to indicate that what we think we see is not always what we see. This entire portion is referring to the Realm of the Illusion.

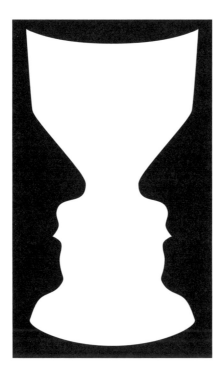

Everything we read here does not make sense from the perspective of the Tree of Knowledge. This is what the Bible is teaching us. The consciousness of "Show me and then I will believe it," or "Seeing is believing," is a fallacy that has become embedded within most of us. But if whatever we see is an illusion, why do we believe in it? In any interaction we can always validate our own actions. The smarter one is the more validation one can come up with.

If we are still holding onto the physicality, the rational mind, and if we believe that this is all we possess, then we possess zero—here today, gone tomorrow. How many of us have been familiar with healthy people who are so robust and then have a "sudden" heart attack that seemingly came out of nowhere? All of these things are here today, gone tomorrow. This is what the portion of Miketz and the entire conversation between the brothers and Joseph is teaching us: here today, gone tomorrow. Why does it disappear? Because, if it involves chaos; it is not real.

If we do not deal with the physical reality we live in, this brings misery. On a rational, physical level, why did Joseph not tell his father he was alive? We do not ask the question. Even about life, we do not ask questions. But how do we expect to get answers if we do not ask the questions?

Suddenly we forget the validation for why we think the way we do. This is why the Bible says Joseph remembered his dream; it is only to indicate that this physical reality cannot be understood unless we take into account many lifetimes, not just that particular moment in time. We cannot have any understanding of what is happening at this moment if this moment is all we direct our attention to.

There is no question that this notion is awesome and profound because it means embarking on a whole new way of life, a whole new way of thinking to grasp the fact that every time something happens it is illusionary. If we direct our consciousness to one time frame, we are living in the life of illusions, and we cannot expect, with all the teachings and tools of Kabbalah, to overcome chaos. It is impossible. We have then opted to live in the world of illusion, which, by the way, does not mean we do not exist. We do exist, but we exist in multiple lifetimes, going beyond lifetimes, beyond this moment in time, all the way back to the beginning of Creation.

Beresheet 43:1 Now the famine was still severe in the land. 2 So when they had eaten all the grain they had brought from Egypt, their father said to them, "Go back and buy us a little more food." 3 But Judah said to him, "The man warned us solemnly, 'You will not see my face again unless your brother is with you.' 4 If you will send our brother along with us, we will go down and buy food for you. 5 But if you will not send him, we will not go down, because the man said to us, 'You will not see my face again unless your brother is with you.' " 6 Israel asked, "Why did you bring this trouble on me by telling the man you had another brother?" 7 They replied, "The man questioned us closely about ourselves and our family. 'Is your father still living?' he asked us. 'Do you have another brother?' We simply answered his questions. How were we to know he would say, 'Bring your brother down here'?" 8 Then Judah said to Israel his father, "Send the boy along with me and we will go at once, so that we and you and our children may live and not die. 9 I myself will guarantee his safety; you can hold me personally responsible for him. If I do not bring him back to you and set him here before you, I will bear the blame before you all my life. 10 As it is, if we had not delayed, we could have gone and returned twice." 11 Then their father Israel said to them, "If it must be, then do this: Put some of the best products of the land in your bags and take them down to the man as a gift—a little balm and a little honey, some spices and myrrh, some pistachio nuts and almonds. 12 Take double the amount of silver with you, for you must return the silver that was put back into the mouths of your sacks. Perhaps it was a mistake. 13 Take your brother also and go back to the man at once. 14 And may God Almighty grant you mercy before the man so that he will let your other brother and Benjamin come back with you. As for me, if I am bereaved of my children, I am bereaved." 15 So the men took the gifts and double the amount of silver, and Benjamin also. They hurried down to Egypt and presented themselves to Joseph. 16 When Joseph saw Benjamin with them, he said to the steward of his house, "Take these men to my house, slaughter an animal and prepare dinner; they are to eat with me at noon." 17 The man did as Joseph told him and took the men to Joseph's house. 18 Now the men were frightened when they were taken to his house. They thought, "We were brought here because of the silver that was put back into our sacks the first time. He wants to attack us and overpower us and seize us as slaves and take our donkeys." 19 So they went up to Joseph's steward and spoke to him at the entrance to the house. 20 "Please sir," they said, "we came down here the first time to buy food. 21 But at the place where we stopped for the night we opened our sacks and each of us found his silver—the exact weight—in the mouth of his sack. So we have brought it back with us. 22 We have also brought additional silver with us to buy food. We don't know who put our silver in our sacks." 23 "It's all right," he said. "Don't be afraid. Your God, the God of your father, has given you treasure in your sacks; I received your silver." Then he brought Simeon out to them. 24 The steward took the men into Joseph's house, gave them water to wash their feet and provided fodder for their donkeys. 25 They prepared their gifts for Joseph's arrival at noon, because they had heard that they were to eat there. 26 When Joseph came home, they presented to him the gifts they had brought into the house, and they bowed down before him to the ground. 27 He asked them how they were, and then he said, "How is your aged father you told me about? Is he still living?" 28 They replied, "Your servant our father is still alive and well." And they bowed low to pay him honor. 29 As he looked about and saw his brother Benjamin, his own mother's son, he asked, "Is this your youngest brother, the one you told me about?" And he said, "God be gracious to you, my son." 30 Deeply moved at the sight of his brother, Joseph hurried out and looked for a place to weep. He went into his private room and wept there. 31 After he had washed his face, he came out and, controlling himself, said, "Serve the food." 32 They served him by himself, the brothers by themselves, and the Egyptians who ate with him by themselves, because Egyptians could not eat with Hebrews, for that is detestable to Egyptians. 33 The men had been seated before him in the order of their ages, from the firstborn to the youngest; and they looked at each other in astonishment. 34 When portions were served to them from Joseph's table, Benjamin's portion was five times as much as anyone else's. So they feasted and drank freely with him.

Beresheet 44:1 Now Joseph gave these instructions to the steward of his house: "Fill the men's sacks with as much food as they can carry, and put each man's silver in the mouth of his sack. 2 Then put my cup, the silver one, in the mouth of the youngest one's sack, along with the silver for his grain." And he did as Joseph said. 3 As morning dawned, the men were sent on their way with their donkeys. 4 They had not gone far from the city when Joseph said to his steward, "Go after those men at once, and when you catch up with them, say to them, 'Why have you repaid good with evil? 5 Isn't this the cup my master drinks from and also uses for divination? This is a wicked thing you have done.' " 6 When he caught up with them, he repeated these words to them. 7 But they said to him, "Why does my lord say such things? Far be it from your servants to do anything like that! 8 We even brought back to you from the land of Canaan the silver we found inside the mouths of our sacks. So why would we steal silver or gold from your master's house? 9 If any of your servants is found to have it, he will die; and the rest of us will become my lord's slaves." 10 "Very well, then," he said, "let it be as you say. Whoever is found to have it will become my slave; the rest of you will be free from blame." 11 Each of them quickly lowered his sack to the ground and opened it. 12 Then the steward proceeded to search, beginning with the oldest and ending with the youngest. And the cup was found in Benjamin's sack. 13 At this, they tore their clothes. Then they all loaded their donkeys and returned to the city. 14 Joseph was still in the house when Judah and his brothers came in and they threw themselves to the ground before him. 15 Joseph said to them, "What is this you have done? Don't you know that a man like me can find things out by divination?" 16 "What can we say to my lord?" Judah replied. "What can we say? How can we prove our innocence? God has uncovered your servants' guilt. We are now my lord's slaves—we ourselves and the one who was found to have the cup." 17 But Joseph said, "Far be it from me to do such a thing! Only the man who was found to have the cup will become my slave. The rest of you, go back to your father in peace."

Making Sense of this Story

Yet again, we have another section of the Bible that is incomprehensible without the Zohar. The "years of famine" are upon the world, and Jacob, hearing that there was food in Egypt, sent ten of his sons there, excluding Benjamin, to purchase grain.

Joseph and Benjamin are Jacob's two sons from Rachel, the wife he loved most, so he would not want anything to happen to Benjamin.

When they arrive in Egypt, Joseph recognizes them. When Joseph spoke to them, he used an interpreter, so it appeared that he did not understand what they said but he heard what they were saying among themselves. Then Yehuda (Eng. Judah) brings Benjamin back with him to Egypt. The question is: Was Joseph seeking revenge when he sent the brothers back with his cup in Benjamin's bag? What did Joseph want? What about his father? His father was in pain every day Benjamin was not at home. Joseph decreed that Benjamin would be a slave to him forever and thus had to remain in Egypt. This is how the portion of Miketz ends. What we have come to understand is the need to go deeper into the biblical text. This story does not make sense unless we interpret it through the Zohar.

One cannot understand the Bible without the Zohar. I realized years ago that Bible study is not just about intellectual understanding. What the circumstances of this story really signify is the nature of consciousness. Every day, every year, we find ourselves in a situation where we are out of control and where people are willing to accept substitutes for control. We are not here to judge if one should settle for less—not even Moses can tell us to keep going this way. The Kabbalah Centres concern themselves with providing kabbalistic tools. We are here to share information, and not to judge what a person does with this information.

Conclusion

The reason the brothers were in chaos is because Benjamin was found to be a thief, and they had promised their father that nothing would happen to him. Immediately they thought that Rachel's other son would be lost. If we cannot raise ourselves to the level of understanding what life is really about then, when we are in those moments of chaos, all is lost. Did Joseph permit this chaos? No. It was not for Joseph to decide. This universe has rules and principles. Thus when something of a chaotic nature falls upon us it is because, either in prior lifetimes or in this lifetime, we have committed a violation. It is our own personal problem no matter how we justify our behavior or blame others for it. In this case, is Joseph to blame? Had Joseph not planted the cup in Benjamin's sack there would have been no problem.

Just as we can say this about Joseph, we can say it about ourselves, too. We can always justify our own errors, claiming not to be responsible. In our minds, someone else still contributes to our chaos. This is the trap that prevents us from letting go of this illusory reality.

There is nothing in this physical universe that escapes the idea of here today, gone tomorrow. Yet we do not wish to let go of it. We do not let go of the Satan's stranglehold on us.

There is nothing that goes on in our lives that is random, whether we are aware of all its implications or not. No one is arbitrarily stricken by chaos. These are the rules. But no one says we must believe or abide in them. The Zohar presents the rules of the universe, and no one says you have to accept them. The principal is that this universe is not governed by the chaotic universe; it is governed by the Flawless Universe, and we all aspire and hope to find ourselves in the Flawless Universe, which is beyond chaos, beyond time, space, and motion.

BOOK OF BERESHEET:

Portion of Vayigash

PORTION OF VAYIGASH

Beresheet 44:18 Then Judah came close to him and said: "Please, my lord, let your servant speak a word to my lord. Do not be angry with your servant, though you are equal to Pharaoh himself.

Judah (Yehuda) Came Close to Joseph

Yehuda comes to speak to Joseph, to plead on behalf of his brothers, and Joseph continues the pretense that he does not know them. This brings more suffering to both his brothers and his father. Was it revenge? Is this what Joseph had in mind? The Zohar says, however, that there are two concepts that would absolutely dispute this kind of thinking. Following the incident with the wife of Potiphar—who attempted to seduce him, but he resisted, performing the restriction necessary to bring about a new name for himself—Yosef became haTzadik, Joseph the Righteous.

The Zohar cannot entertain the fact that Joseph could possibly have been seeking revenge against his brothers. So what does all this mean? For answers to these questions we turn to the Zohar, which, as Rav Isaac Luria (the Ari) explains, opens up some of the channels, as well as some of our personal hidden potential. By virtue of just reading the Zohar, we make connections immediately. The extent of the connection we make, however, depends on each individual. Merely by reading the words, without even understanding the Aramaic, we immediately make a connection to cosmic consciousness, a level of sub-consciousness, of the ninety-two percent of us. Now you might consider this illusionary. For me, ninety-two percent represents more than the eight percent capacity with which medical science says we function. I, for one, refuse to be satisfied with eight percent, and am going to make every effort to connect to that level that is beyond eight percent. At one time, Sephardim in particular were considered very illogical and irrational people because they dealt in the realm of the ninety-two percent. They would simply read the Zohar without necessarily understanding what the Zohar was about; but this was what brought to them the Golden Age of Spain, considered the greatest period in Jewish history since the Destruction of the Temple. I would like to follow in their footsteps, and maybe also acquire that consciousness beyond the eight percent rational mind. Therefore, I will always read the Aramaic in the Zohar when I study. I also believe that by scanning the Aramaic words of the Zohar, we open up a completely new channel of information that permits all of us to understand—beyond the level of the rational physical reality—what the Zohar is going to teach us in reference to the questions we have just raised. The Zohar says:

"Then Judah came near to him." (Beresheet 44:18) Rav Elazar opened the discussion with the verse, "You are our Father, though Abraham be ignorant of us, and Israel acknowledge us not. You, Lord, are our Father, our Redeemer; Your name is from everlasting." (Yeshayah 63:16) This verse has already been explained. Yet, come and behold, when the Holy One, blessed be He, created the world, He did, each day, the work befitting it. When the sixth day arrived—the time for Adam to be created—the Torah came before Him and said, "Adam, whom You want to create, will provoke You. Unless You curb Your wrath, it would be better for him not to be created." The Holy One, blessed be He, asked, "Am I called long-suffering for no reason?" All was created through the medium of the Torah, and constructed by means of the Torah. AND AS THE TORAH BEGINS WITH THE

LETTER *BET*, SO WAS THE WORLD CREATED WITH THE LETTER *BET*. For before the Holy One, blessed be He, created the world—THE NUKVA—all the letters were presented before Him one by one, in reverse order.
—Zohar, Vayigash 1:1-2

From this passage in the Zohar, we learn that our entire universe was created by the Hebrew letters. Therefore, if the Hebrew letters represent the seed of Creation, they are inclusive of the Creation, containing all the universes and galaxies. This means that within the Torah Scroll is contained the entire universe, opened up for all to control. When we connect with the letters as the Torah is read, in essence, we have taken control of a good part of the universe. If this is the case, then we begin to understand why, from a kabbalistic point of view, humanity appears to be in total disarray with the universe, having no control over our environment. For just as we can control this entire universe and make use of it, as well as make use of all the forces within it to enhance our lives, so do we have the same opportunity and decision-making capacity to create disarray. It is not the Creator who provides this abnormal universe we live in, but rather it is through our own actions that everything we see before us has transpired.

To understand the story of the sale of Joseph and his reaction to his brothers, we will discuss these two parts of the Torah, the parchment and the inscribed Hebrew letters in it. The Zohar explains that, contrary to what we think, the parchment is the power and the letters are merely channels by which the power of the parchment becomes expressed. Just as thoughts become manifest through the words, so the force of the parchment becomes expressed by the Hebrew letters. There is the physical expression, observed by the letters, and then there is the parchment, the metaphysical, all-powerful energy system of the entire universe.

The Zohar says that everything, including humankind, is created by these Hebrew letters. Therefore, it only follows that we, ourselves, also have two parts: the soul and the body. Unfortunately, we are not always in control of both parts. One minute we can be full of ecstasy and the next minute we are depressed or angry. In other words, we are schizophrenic all the time. The only difference between those people who are locked up in institutions and those of us on the "outside" is that we on the outside somehow manage to deal with those around us. But if we could not deal with others, we would be classified as schizophrenic—since this disorder is characterized by a loss of contact with others and the environment. For most people, daily life means today we are up, tomorrow we are down. Or this hour we are up, and the next hour we are down. I am not discussing the person who behaves irrationally. I am referring to most people who are considered to be normal, yet still have their ups and downs within each day—and we think this is perfectly normal. But is it? The two parts to us—the physical body and the metaphysical soul—are what create the ups and downs.

The Zohar declares that Joseph's ten brothers, the ones who sold him into slavery, were Chariots of the signs of the zodiac. They were physical people whose metaphysical aspect had complete access to the cosmos, to all that was, all that is, and all that will ever be. These people were very much physical and connected to this physical realm, but they also never lost contact with the cosmos, meaning they were always totally connected with yesterday, today, and tomorrow. Nevertheless, in a parallel universe, this metaphysical part exists in every individual. What the brothers had acquired was not something that came through experience or through study, through prayer, or through other mediums. They were simply born that way, born connected to this world of Malchut—the base world of mud—but at the same time possessing total cosmic consciousness. They could be in both places at the same time and not be affected by the ups and downs. These were not people with robotic-consciousness, which is precisely why it is difficult to fathom that people of such elevated spiritual consciousness could sell their own brother. The Zohar provides us with a clue to what is really taking place. There is something far deeper going on, far deeper than a superficial tale about the sale of Joseph.

Human beings who have no control can be like Jekyll and Hyde—two opposing personalities in the same person. Joseph and his brothers were conscious people, operating on two levels at the same time, in two parallel universes. On one level, they were Chariots of the constellations and could look down from above, knowing what exists within the stars. They saw the entire picture from beginning to end. They saw the end result—that there would have to be bondage in Egypt. The Zohar explains the reason for this is because certain souls failed in their *tikkun* (spiritual correction) process, these souls being the generations of the Flood and the Tower of Babel. Because of this failure, they had to incarnate in the world once more. These souls would have to go through the suffering of bondage in Egypt to create the right circumstances for a *tikkun*. The Zohar explains that in this physical dimension it is human activity that creates the movie we experience. If we make selfish choices, the end result is so much negative cosmic energy. A holocaust is merely the result of humanity's prior actions because we are really in total control of the universe. Whether we produce a picture of harmony or a picture of total chaos depends solely upon us.

The Zohar explains that Jacob's ten sons knew very well what was happening when they sold Joseph, and thus it was not with malice that they did this. Then why does the Bible in Genesis 37:4 state, *vayisnu oto*, which is translated to mean "they hated him"? I cannot feasibly conceive that people who are Chariots, who represent the totality of control over the cosmos, would lower themselves to do something that none of us would probably ever dream of doing.

The Zohar tells us to never accept this corrupt translation because there is no aspect of hatred within a Chariot. So what does *vayisnu oto* really mean then? It means there was no connection between the two: Joseph represented the cosmic consciousness of Yesod, of Zeir Anpin; the brothers were in the realm of Malchut. So Joseph and his brothers were in different realms. Yet because the brothers were Chariots, they saw tomorrow and knew that all those souls were destined to come down to Egypt and be in bondage there. This was the physical reality or Malchut procedure—and it was inevitable.

The answer to why Joseph did not inform his father he was alive for 17 years is found in the same explanation as that given for the sale of Joseph. Jacob and Joseph were Chariots, meaning they were part of the Celestial system. They were channels for the way humankind was to evolve, and thus they emanated the way their *tikkuns* were to happen. These were not people like us. For most of us who are not chariots and, therefore, not connected to the 99 Percent Reality, we have to live in this mundane world.

We have been educated with a philosophy that says what we experience with the five senses is the world of reality. Yet along come the scientists, who have told us of late that the physical reality is an illusion. So there are two parts, the illusionary Malchut level where action takes place, and the Tree of Life Reality where yesterday, today, and tomorrow are one. The Zohar is teaching us there are two parallel universes operating at the same time, and that there are two separate and distinct parallel universes within all of us—namely the soul and the body.

With this understanding of two parallel universes, we can appreciate that Joseph, who is Yesod, knew he would interfere in the process. If he had returned to Israel and made there a connection with that land, with the Malchut, the exile in Egypt would never have taken place. It would be all over. Where would the opportunity be for the souls of the generations of the Flood and the Tower of Babel to return, to live again in this world of illusion, and thereby make their *tikkun*? It never would have happened.

The Zohar cautions us never to give advice to a person, even if we are asked, because we might be interfering with their *tikkun*, with that person's free will. We can only do this if we consider the individual as ourselves—and we must truly feel the person as if they are us. When you are in the sharing process, the individual must be as you. In the sharing process, there have to be equal opposites, meaning an equally sincere Desire to Receive that which is being shared. Joseph knew there was a process here, a process of new souls who would ultimately have to come down; so he did not return to Israel. Jacob was also of this high consciousness. If this was the case, what then caused suffering?

Jacob was not suffering in any way we would understand. He was suffering because he was separated from Joseph in the metaphysical realm—meaning that Jacob, who is Tiferet, had to remain in exile and could not become one unified whole with Joseph, who is Yesod.

It is crucial to understand this vital aspect of non-interference. No one, not even Joseph, has a right to interfere with someone else's *tikkun* process. Who are we to consider ourselves an authority on how one person should or should not behave?

When Joseph makes himself known to his brothers, it does not contradict what we have just learned from the Zohar. Jacob had no pain, yet he also experienced pain. If we ask for more pain, we can experience pain but on entirely other level—in fact we realize the paradox of pain, how it slowly but surely disappears. It is a great feeling. You should all try it. If you have a bad toothache, try it. You can run to the medicine chest, which is one way to handle it. Or you can run to your dentist. We are talking here only about the pain aspect of a toothache—an infection is something completely different, and for that you need to see a doctor or dentist immediately. Although we are dealing with an illusionary Malchut level, nevertheless it has its place in the *tikkun* process. Physically, the body exists. Even though it is part of the illusionary world, we do need this aspect of Malchut, we need both rails of the train tracks to run on them smoothly. They both must always be there because this is the only way we can experience free will and predetermination. If there was no body, there would be no free will nor any predetermination. We would be at a robotic level of consciousness. There would never again be the removal of Bread of Shame—which is the principal reason why we are here in the first place.

The ends never justify the means, though. Therefore, despite the fact that these ten sons of Jacob were Chariots of the cosmos, they still operated in parallel universes. One universe follows the rule of Malchut, the physical 1 Percent Realm, and the other universe follows the rule of the Chariots, the 99 Percent Reality. In the Malchut realm, Joseph is sold because of the *tikkun* process—there has to be bondage in Egypt and an exodus. Nevertheless, it still involved the sale of a brother, and for that 1 Percent illusionary process a price had to be paid. So there is no contradiction in viewing the sons of Jacob as Chariots. Yet on the 1 Percent Level they had to pay a price—and that price was death. It was necessary for them to reincarnate as the ten martyrs who were killed by the Romans at the time of the destruction of the Second Holy Temple. So too was it with Jacob. He experienced physical pain but was also totally conscious of what was going on.

This is what we teach in our Centres: how to connect with cosmic consciousness, meaning that yesterday, today, and tomorrow are all here now. With this portion, we are really discussing how to become masters of our own destiny. How many of us can say we control everything? I mean, the weather is not going to bother me, not going to spoil my week, and earthquakes will not interfere with my daily life. Crime, too, will not interfere with me. Who can say this? For most of us, the environment is so overwhelming and all-pervasive that we make very few decisions of our own that are truly independent of it. In other words, we are governed by television and by advertisements that dictate everything, from the food we eat to the clothes we wear. We are not free people because most of the time these extraneous things govern how we behave. Everything dealing with the physical illusionary aspect is what creates bondage. Yehuda wanted to interfere with the whole exile and exodus. Knowing he was going to suffer, he wanted to change the outcome, he wanted to connect with Yesod (Joseph) because Yesod represents *Ge'ula* (Redemption)—the 99 Percent Reality. We learn from these three words—*vayigash elav Yehuda*—that Malchut can reach up into the dimension of Zeir Anpin. Yehuda went close to Joseph because he wanted to elevate Malchut and connect the two parallel universes.

When we pray the Amida connection, *Ge'ula* (Freedom or Redemption) is what we should focus on because when we have freedom we do not have all the pressures that force us into situations we do not necessarily want to be in. Freedom encompasses intelligence and everything else necessary, our health and welfare—freedom encompasses all. The Zohar says, with *vayigash elav Yehuda*, that once all these Chariots have established the possibility for linkup with another dimension, we can all do it, and then we can actually all be free.

The Zohar says if we only read the Bible story superficially nothing is revealed because in almost every verse there is either a contradiction or else some kind of ridiculous statement. Why has this been going on for 3,400 years? It seems as if we have forgotten the importance of the Zohar. Never in 50 years, have I been without a Zohar. Yet we do tend to forget its importance. This is the only answer.

Why do we persist in trying to understand the Bible as a literal text when it makes absolutely no sense to us at all? The Zohar asks a simpler question: What do the first three words contain? The very first words of a chapter are the Sefira of Keter, the beginning, and they always contain everything else that follows. I like to take the Zohar's approach to this, so when I want to know what a portion has to tell us, I look at the first words. Yet, in this case, the words seem totally confusing and mystifying—at least they do as far as extracting any deeper meaning goes. Where can we find the motif, the indicator of what is to come? It can be found by those who take the time to search in the first verse—and especially by those who read the Zohar.

Herein lies the whole secret of what the Kabbalah Centre is about, and why we have been condemned for nearly 100 years—although we have been spoken about for both good and ill. Our purpose is to bring this chaotic, painful, and suffering world into that universe known as Zeir Anpin, which is the Tree of Life Reality, the Flawless Universe. Our aim is to bring together Malchut with Zeir Anpin, so we can alleviate chaos, if not remove it from our lives altogether.

As I state every Shabbat, without the Torah reading, the week will not be free of chaos. We cannot do it ourselves, no matter how brilliant we are. While we may eliminate chaos from our personal lives, without this entire world reading the Zohar, none of us— whether on our own or collectively with all the Kabbalah Centres on Earth— none of us can bring together Zeir Anpin with Malchut and thereby eliminate pain and suffering. We need all the people of the world.

19 "My lord asked his servants, 'Do you have a father or a brother?' 20 And we answered, 'We have an aged father, and there is a young son born to him in his old age. His brother is dead, and he is the only one of his mother's sons left, and his father loves him.' 21 Then you said to your servants, 'Bring him down to me so I can see him for myself.' 22 And we said to my lord, 'The boy cannot leave his father; if he leaves him, his father will die.' 23 But you told your servants, 'Unless your youngest brother comes down with you, you will not see my face again.' 24 When we went back to your servant my father, we told him what my lord had said. 25 Then our father said, 'Go back and buy a little more food.' 26 But we said, 'We cannot go down. Only if our youngest brother is with us will we go. We cannot see the man's face unless our youngest brother is with us.' 27 Your servant my father said to us, 'You know that my wife bore me two sons. 28 One of them went away from me,' and I said, 'He has surely been torn to pieces. And I have not seen him since. 29 If you take this one from me too and harm comes to him, you will bring my gray head down to the grave in misery.' 30 So now, if the boy is not with us when I go back to your servant my father and if my father, whose life is closely bound up with the boy's life, 31 sees that the boy isn't there, he will die. Your servants will bring the gray head of our father down to the grave in sorrow. 32 Your servant guaranteed the boy's safety to my father. I

said, 'If I do not bring him back to you, I will bear the blame before you, my father, all my life!' 33 Now then, please let your servant remain here as my lord's slave in place of the boy, and let the boy return with his brothers. 34 How can I go back to my father if the boy is not with me? No! Do not let me see the misery that would come upon my father."

The Meeting of Malchut and Yesod

Why does Yehuda repeat the entire story as if he is pleading these circumstances to obtain the court's mercy? The whole thing seems utterly ridiculous. The Zohar says this section is here to teach us that this is our nature and the way we all behave. The reason Yehuda repeats everything is because the Bible is telling us that if we do not *vayigash alav Yehuda*, if we do not do this together—bring Malchut closer to Zeir Anpin—chaos will not leave the world, not ever. Everyone must be included. The Jews have to be aware of the Arabs, and the Arabs have to be aware of the Jews, and this applies to everyone everywhere there is conflict, everywhere there is pain and suffering. Each individual has to learn to be conscious of the humanity of others. That is what Yehuda is talking about—and the repetition of the story serves to remove chaos.

Why should Joseph be interested in Yehuda's retelling of this story? On a material level, Vayigash is entirely about the meeting between Yehuda and Joseph, and later the reunion between Jacob and Joseph. On a spiritual level, it is about the meeting between the Malchut of the Tree of Knowledge and the Yesod of the Tree of Life. This is a meeting of two worlds, and it has to do with conflict, on one hand, and convergence on the other. Convergence is always associated with conflict. Using the example of a lightbulb, conflict creates the connection of two polarities, which are in opposition to the current.

Whenever there is conflict, there is much Light to be revealed, which in this case is connected to Yehuda, who is Malchut, and Joseph, who is Yesod. We, too, carry on about our own preoccupations about settling old scores, not willing to change. We are not ready to move away from the cesspool and, if we finally get out of the mud, we bring the cesspool and the garbage along with us. To really be with the Light we must change.

I associate this matter of conflict in Vayigash with a light that suddenly burns brighter before it is extinguished. This is what happens before a man's death; suddenly he feels relief, he feels much better, and everyone thinks he is now on the road to recovery—but then suddenly he is dead. This is the power of Satan, who causes an illusion that looks like the Light of life. With this biblical portion, we can wash away the illusion with the power of the Tree of Life. We have to be serious in our intention to get rid of the chaos we create. The desire to settle old scores and so on is the way we take Satan with us, and he will never leave us alone.

Yehuda's repetition of what has already occurred comprises a good proportion of this section. The Zohar asks why the Bible tells us "Judah came close." Why not simply say "he said"? In brief, the Zohar states this portion is about revealing that which is concealed—which is also the purpose of this whole universe. Yehuda represents Malchut, and Joseph is our connection to Yesod— our connection to being able to tap into and draw the sustenance that this universe and everything in it requires to grow. Joseph represents Yesod, and that is why we have his picture ever-present, so he is not just an individual but a sphere from which we receive all of our sustenance. By sustenance we mean the Lightforce of God that fulfills all forms of lack or need.

When we experience a form of chaos, such as ill health, Satan has his ways of helping us forget about the personal wars we wage, which are so miniscule compared with what humanity as a whole faces today. Some people take Prozac, others prefer war. I do not want to minimize the tragedy of war, but in reference to what people suffer every day all around the world, war is actually very minimal. This is especially so for those who are not close to people who perished in war. Yehuda outlined the different ways his family was affected by chaos, when chaos came upon them. And the Zohar explains that the reason the Bible says "and he drew close to him" is because there is only one way we can remove chaos from our lives. It does not matter in what form this chaos strikes. Someone may find a cure for their illness, which may seem to disappear—but it does not disappear; it comes back in a different form.

Chaos is the absence of Light. Removing chaos means not having its influence in our lives. This is a concept that humankind should be able to grasp but we need to understand it is not that chaos is removed from just one area. When we turn on a light the darkness disappears. Where does it go? Darkness does not disappear from this world—the proof is that it returns. That is the teaching of this reading. If all we hope to achieve is the removal of one form of chaos, it is an exercise in futility.

There is only one way to remove chaos and all forms of tragedy from the world, and that is when Malchut becomes one with Yesod. Therefore, this long story, which is repeated here, shows us life is a constant struggle, and that physical effort alone is not able to remove chaos—all it can do is provide temporary relief. It is an illusion that there has been a "full recovery." The doctors will say they got rid of the cancer—and then it recurs. What does that mean? It means the Light went off and on and off again. There is no disappearance of anything, including darkness. Where the darkness is concealed, it does not disappear, and it will come back in another place. Like the magician who makes a pigeon disappear, we can make things disappear but this is just an illusion. It must come back. In the case of an illness, at least the person has some respite for a few years but there is no permanent cure.

The removal of radiation and other toxins, not only in places like Chernobyl but around the United States as well, would cost trillions of dollars, and so we are forced to live with these poisons. The Lightforce of God cannot eliminate physicality. If we remove arsenic from water, do we annihilate the arsenic? No, the arsenic is reduced to levels that are not harmful; it is replaced by a different energy.

We are bringing Malchut in contact with Yesod during this reading by implementing the methodology of Kabbalah through the Bible— there is no other method to remove chaos. There is no other way to remove the physical obstruction without the combining of Malchut with Yesod. The study of Kabbalah and the 72 Names of God are ways to connect Yesod with the Malchut. It is not easy, and no one claims it is, but what the Zohar is saying here is that there is no way of removing any form of chaos so conclusively that it does not return—no way, that is, unless we have the absolute conviction and certainty that it will *not* come back. We are faced with many problems that seem insurmountable but with the technology of Kabbalah we have the tools for the task at hand.

Beresheet 45:1 Then Joseph could no longer control himself before all his attendants, and he cried out, "Have everyone leave my presence!" So, there was no one with Joseph when he made himself known to his brothers. 2 And he wept so loudly that the Egyptians heard him, and Pharaoh's household heard about it. 3 Joseph said to his brothers, "I am Joseph! Is my father still living?" But his brothers were not able to answer him, because they were terrified at his presence. 4 Then Joseph said to his brothers, "Come close to me." When they had done so, he said, "I am your brother Joseph, the one you sold into Egypt! 5 And now, do not be distressed and do not be angry with yourselves for selling me here, because it was to save lives that God sent me ahead of you."

Joseph and His Brothers

Joseph revealed himself to his brothers and asked if their father was still alive. Joseph then invested all his energy in bringing Jacob to Egypt. Why is it that Joseph was suddenly concerned about his father? We need to know that every other person is a part of us.

It took 34 verses to explain what had already been stated in Miketz. Then the Bible says Joseph could control himself no longer, so he told them to take all the attendants out because he did not want anyone there when, weeping, he admitted he was their brother. The Bible says everyone heard it, the whole country heard it, including the house of Pharaoh. Joseph said to his brothers, "I am Joseph," and of course his brothers were in a state of shock. What we see from this following verse is that there are different levels of protection. Each activity of the Kabbalah Centres is concerned with one idea: To bring this chaotic reality in contact with the world of Yesod, the world of Joseph. This happened the moment Yehuda drew near to Joseph. When this connection was made, Joseph could no longer conceal the fact that he was their brother. Why did he disclose himself now and not before, when the brothers were suffering the torment of their story? It had to occur after this connection was made because turmoil and concealment cannot coexist. In a given situation, if any doubt remains, then we do not truly believe that the contact we made did indeed remove the chaos. Here contact with Yesod was made so the chaos of concealment could not continue, and so Joseph was forced to tell them he was their brother. This is how the universal system works. It is very profound, and yet there is no other system I know of that works.

We would like every person to scan the Zohar because the moment the Zohar is read or scanned there is the removal of a certain aspect of darkness. The Kabbalah Centres have done so much over the past 40 years. We are creating a climate of spirituality each and every day by scanning the Zohar. Of course, if you are a user of the Internet you can scan the Zohar there. Every day, I hear about miracles, and I am not talking about miracles we cannot observe with the senses.

We have here, with the reading of Vayigash, an opportunity to bring Malchut together with Yesod. This is an opportunity to remove chaos instantly, without having to look behind us to see if it has really disappeared. We can have a certainty that it has been removed.

The Subtlety of the Tikkun (Spiritual Correction) Process

What is the meaning of the phrase "Joseph could not restrain himself any longer from revealing his identity"? This verse has nothing to do with Joseph, it is about Zeir Anpin releasing this power. When the right time comes and we are ready for it, Zeir Anpin takes over with the correct action.

Why do we ask for *rachamim* (mercy)? What about the rule of Bread of Shame? Instead of blaming and justifying, take responsibility. There is a *tikkun* process at work, which means there is no such thing as a person suffering forever. There is an end to suffering. There is a process by which *tikkun* takes place, and then *rachamim* (mercy) happens when Zeir Anpin takes over.

But who decided that the brothers' *tikkun* was over? Were they "forgiven" because of Joseph's level of connection or was it because Joseph was the victim? Do we look back and think about our own negativity, and in that moment recognize we have done something to create the chaos we experience?

What happened after the brothers sold Joseph? In the 17 years that followed, Yehuda saw the death of his wife and two of his sons, and the entire family experienced famine and had to go to Egypt in search of food. Did they not think about what they had done to bring these things upon themselves? We have to see the darkness and negativity in ourselves, and then realize it is our responsibility to do our own *tikkun*. But this is very difficult to achieve.

How many people have attended a Kabbalah Centre for many years and still not come to a realization that they must accept responsibility for their personal situation? There is no *tikkun* made if we do not think we have done something to cause the chaos in our lives. Most still want to blame others for what they go through.

It took the brothers 17 years to realize the reason for their misfortunes. Chaos came into their lives time and again until they understood that this happened because they sold their brother into slavery. The brothers were *tzadikim*, Chariots, but they were also regular people. Was this all God's will? Did God want to see suffering and pain? Of course not. It is an opportunity to open up the channel of mercy or *rachamim*.

Is there such a thing as the consequence for a violation that never ends? Even a serious punishment has an end to its *tikkun*. And we can shorten the *tikkun* process through Kabbalah technology. To shorten the process we must take advantage of all the moments where we can get extra Light to do our *tikkun*, and then accept responsibility, thereby closing that chapter.

The inspiration in this reading is that everything could be different tomorrow. This is such a powerful Shabbat and a great opportunity for us. All we have to do is open up a gate in ourselves. But it is difficult to rid ourselves of the petty thought, the thought that we are still a little right. In an argument, why not just say, "You are right and I am wrong"? What would happen? It would help us greatly to finish with our *tikkun* process. We need to take responsibility for our actions and for everything that comes to us. Sometimes it may be from a past life. We have to ask ourselves what we did to bring this situation about—even if it is a positive outcome.

People give to charity. Then they experience chaos and say, "I was so good and kind this last year. What happened? Why are things not going right?" It is because we have to pay our dues little by little through the *tikkun* process. This reading gives us a great opportunity to clear up our *tikkun*.

I just want to repeat again that this is an opportunity that only comes once a year—the opportunity of what we can accomplish when we acknowledge that whatever we have in our lives, whatever is taking place, we are responsible for it. This is probably the most difficult task for humankind to tackle. The reason we always seem to be back at the same point is because we have not been able to accomplish accepting responsibility.

Every negative aspect in our lives is only there because of our own actions. If we attain that elevated state of mind for just an hour or two, we can access the gates that are literally opened up for us on this Shabbat.

When the Bible says Joseph could no longer control himself, what really happened was that the gates of Malchut opened. Yehuda was prepared to accept the one crucial understanding—that we are responsible for everything negative in our lives. If we still cannot accept this idea that the fault is ours, we have wasted our time and this valuable text.

We need all the Light that can come from this portion. I appeal to everyone to try out these lessons here for an hour and a half. If we can do that, we will have opened up gates of abundance that have previously been closed to us.

Joseph and Foundation

The Zohar says:

> Another man stood and quoted, "And Joseph said to his brothers, 'Come near to me, I pray you.' And they came near. And he said..." (Beresheet 45:4) AND HE ASKED, "Why did he have to call them, as they were close by?" AND HE REPLIED, "Because when he told them, 'I am Joseph your brother' they were astonished, because they saw him as elevated royalty. So Joseph told them, 'I gained this kingdom because of this, REFERRING TO CIRCUMCISION.

Come near to me.' They came nearer, and he showed them
the sign of the Covenant, the circumcision. He said, 'Because
I have preserved the Covenant, I have earned this kingdom.'"
—Zohar, Lech Lecha 36:398

The male sex organ is Sefirat Yesod. Sefirat Yesod is indicated here
because Sefirat Yesod is the letter *Vav*. Therefore, the male sex
organ appears as a *Vav* for no other reason than that it represents
the bottled-up energy that is referred to by the code name Yesod
(Foundation). It is called Foundation because wherever this Sefira
is found it is as Joseph. From there flows all the abundance and
blessings the world requires. The narration concerning Joseph in
Egypt being in control and nourishing the entire world is due to
one factor: He is Yesod, and from Yesod all the abundance flows to
Malchut, to our world.

Performing a *brit milah* (circumcision), is to remove the *orla*
(foreskin) because the foreskin is the embodiment of all negative
energy concentrated in one place. As we have discussed previously,
there is no greater concentration of such negative energy anywhere
within the physical body, within this universe, as there is in the
foreskin. It is located in this particular place and nowhere else
because it is Yesod. And wherever there is an opening for energy
to flow, this is where you will find Satan and all of those negative
energy-intelligences that cause trouble for individuals, for society,
for the whole universe. For the same reason, we put a *mezuzah* on
the door post. Satan knows where energy is to be found—and the
highest concentration of energy is to be found in the male sex organ.
This is because there is nothing more powerful than the sperm that
can produce the human race, a power without equal in our universe.
Since this kind of energy flows from the male sex organ, there we
will also find the greatest concentration of negative energy. They
both exist in the same place. As it is with the poison ivy tree, if you
want to know where the cure for its sting lies, it grows on another

tree adjacent to the one with poison ivy. So wherever we find negativity, we will always find its cure of positivity. Thus the reason for circumcision is to remove this high concentration of negative energy contained in the foreskin.

Jacob's Sadness

We shall all benefit from the moment Joseph revealed himself to his brothers. The lesson of Vayigash is to understand that none of us can live alone. When the Bible says Joseph could no longer contain himself, this is to teach us that without the resolution of the separation that exists between Zeir Anpin (Joseph) and Malchut (Yehuda), pain and suffering will never be removed.

If chaos occurs anywhere in the world, it will affect us. I am not a prophet. The reason I have access to this information is because I pursue it. One thing I do know is that chaos will bring everyone down, every human being and every animal, as well as the crops, the fruits and vegetables. We are living in Armageddon right now. If we do not understand this and let sink deep into our consciousness that it is the Zohar, and only the Zohar, together with the reading of the Bible that can remove chaos—if we cannot do this then we have no chance of surviving Armageddon. I challenge one person to tell me that he or she has enjoyed freedom from chaos for one full week or even one full day. We do not experience a chaos-free existence because we are affected by everyone else. Science gave us quantum but many reject this concept too because they do not understand it. But we understand.

Joseph knew his father was in pain for 17 years before he finally revealed himself. Why did it take him this long? Did Joseph love his father or had the long absence made him forget? It is obvious that if Joseph wanted to be rid of his brothers, with his power he could have easily done it. Perhaps his brothers were lying when they told him that if Benjamin did not return their father would unquestionably die?

The Bible is not story-telling here. As the Zohar constantly reminds us, it is foolish to regard it in such a literal way. Yet this misreading of the Bible is all around us. The Zohar discusses the portion at length, something which the commentators find a little difficult. But, if you recall, Joseph's brothers presented him to their father as dead, by bringing his coat smeared with blood and ripped to pieces. When they brought that coat to Jacob, he became sad, which caused him to forget. The Zohar says this sadness caused Jacob to lose the Shechinah. What does this mean? It means he did not maintain his former consciousness. One hears of such things all the time; every day is filled with tragedy. People everywhere have problems that cause them to lose their consciousness. This is why I reiterate that to maintain consciousness we must come every Shabbat and listen to the reading of the Torah Scroll—or at least scan the Zohar every day on our own. Each and every one of us has an obligation to further improve our lives. Those of us who do not have enough consciousness to try to help another individual in this world are liable for what will indubitably come back to haunt them. This is why the Jew is hated—because they say they do not want this obligation.

The Zohar was held back for 3,400 years because it was thought to be better if we did not have the obligation. But it is an obligation we cannot shirk. Anyone who understands the value of the Zohar and yet does not make an effort to spread this great text that can improve people's lives, such people are guilty of the pain and suffering that could have been alleviated or removed from lives. This is what is meant when it is said Jacob forgot. He had a loss of consciousness. If there is no consciousness down here, there is no consciousness in the Flawless Universe.

6 For two years now there has been famine in the land and for the next five years there will not be plowing and reaping. 7 But God sent me ahead of you to preserve for you a remnant on earth and to save your lives by a great deliverance. 8 So then, it was not you who sent me here, but God. He made me father to Pharaoh, lord of his entire household and ruler of all Egypt. 9 Now hurry back to my father and say to him, 'This is what your son Joseph says: God has made me lord of all Egypt. Come down to me; don't delay. 10 You shall live in the region of Goshen and be near me—you, your children and grandchildren, your flocks and herds, and all you have.

Why They Went to Goshen

The reason Jacob and his sons went to the land of Goshen is that Yehuda, Jacob, and Joseph represent the conjunction of Zeir Anpin and Malchut. The word Goshen is derived from the word *vayigash*, which is the connection between Yehuda (Malchut) and Joseph and Jacob (Zeir Anpin), who are both the Central Columns, respectively, of the Upper and Lower Triads of the Magen David (Shield of David). This is how their union becomes manifest. See image on page 85.

TIFERET
Beauty
JACOB

GEVURAH
Judgment
ISAAC

CHESED
Mercy
ABRAHAM

POTENTIAL

MANIFESTATION

HOD
Splendor
AARON

NETZACH
Victory
MOSES

YESOD
Formation
JOSEPH

11 I will provide for you there, because five years of famine are still to come. Otherwise you and your household and all who belong to you will become destitute.' 12 You can see for yourselves, and so can my brother Benjamin, that it is really I who am speaking to you. 13 Tell my father about all the honor accorded me in Egypt and about everything you have seen. And bring my father down here quickly." 14 Then he threw his arms around his brother Benjamin and wept, and Benjamin embraced him, weeping. 15 And he kissed all his brothers and wept over them. Afterward his brothers talked with him. 16 When the news reached Pharaoh's palace that Joseph's brothers had come, Pharaoh and all his officials were pleased. 17 Pharaoh said to Joseph, "Tell your brothers, 'Do this: Load your animals and return to the land of Canaan, 18 and bring your father and your households back to me. I will give you the best of the land of Egypt and you can enjoy the fat of the land.' 19 You are also directed to tell them, 'Do this: Take some carts from Egypt for your children and your wives, and get your father and come. 20 Never mind about your belongings, because the best of all Egypt will be yours.'" 21 So the sons of Israel did this. Joseph gave them carts, as Pharaoh had commanded, and he also gave them provisions for their journey. 22 To each of them he gave new clothing, but to Benjamin he gave three hundred shekels of silver and five sets of clothes. 23 And this is what he sent to his father: ten donkeys

loaded with the best things of Egypt, and ten female donkeys loaded with grain and bread and other provisions for his journey. 24 Then he sent his brothers away, and as they were leaving he said to them, "Don't quarrel on the way!"

Jacob Teaches About Human Nature

Joseph asked his brothers to bring their father to Egypt and just as they were leaving, he told them not to fight on their way back. He said this immediately after telling them who he was so as to relieve their remorse. He told them that the reason he was sold into slavery was so he would interpret Pharaoh's dream and take control during the famine, thus saving the world. Joseph considered this a validation of his being sold into slavery. But at that time the brothers came from a place of hatred and jealousy, so Joseph told them not to fight on the way back. His thought must have been that they would argue still over which of them instigated the selling of Joseph. Although he had just told them there was a higher purpose for all of this, the brothers still had a debt to pay.

What Joseph is teaching us here is that, just as we have, in effect, two ears—one for the words to enter and one for the words to exit—human nature is similarly dual. People have no real appreciation of the things that happen to them. In the same way, many do not value what they receive in the Kabbalah Centres. We have heard people say, "I'll never forget what the Centre has done for me," and then we do not see that individual again. Many people tell us how much they have done for the Centre. Those words are not something you will hear from Karen and I because we are constantly aware of how much the Centre has done for us. We have to remember that ingratitude is right behind us, waiting to come in and take us away.

This section is about the removal of the chaos between Joseph and his brothers. We need to perform actions on a daily basis that will cause Zeir Anpin not to withhold itself any longer but to reveal itself in our lives and create miracles. The Upper World opens to us through the actions we perform and in our taking responsibility for all our actions.

25 So they went up out of Egypt and came to their father Jacob in the land of Canaan. 26 They told him, "Joseph is still alive! In fact, he is ruler of all Egypt." Jacob was stunned; he did not believe them. 27 But when they told him everything Joseph had said to them, and when he saw the carts Joseph had sent to carry him back, the spirit of their father Jacob revived. 28 And Israel said, "I'm convinced! My son Joseph is still alive. I will go and see him before I die."

Beresheet 46:1 So Israel set out with all that was his, and when he reached Beersheba, he offered sacrifices to the God of his father Isaac.

Jacob and Joseph

Jacob said, "I will go and see him before I die" (אלכה ואראנו בטרם אמות). Jacob is in the world for the sake of Tiferet (Beauty) and to create the manifestation of Joseph the Righteous, which is Yesod (Foundation). When Jacob paired with Yesod, one hundred and six years were added to his life so that he could make sacrifices in the name of Isaac on his way to Egypt—Isaac, who had been bound on the altar so there would be less judgment in the world and the children of Israel would be able to get out of Egypt.

**2 And God spoke to Israel in a vision at night
and said, "Jacob! Jacob!" "Here I am," he
replied. 3 "I am God, the God of your father,"
he said. "Do not be afraid to go down to Egypt,
for I will make you into a great nation there.
4 I will go down to Egypt with you, and I will
surely bring you back again. And Joseph's
own hand will close your eyes." 5 Then Jacob
left Beersheba, and Israel's sons took their
father Jacob and their children and their
wives in the carts that Pharaoh had sent to
transport him. 6 They also took with them
their livestock and the possessions they had
acquired in Canaan, and Jacob and all his offspring went to Egypt. 7 He took with him to
Egypt his sons and grandsons and his daughters and granddaughters—all his offspring.**

The Beginning of Exile

We must remember that when Joseph was a slave he was also the
boss because he controlled the household. This is to show us what
appears to be a prison is not necessarily a prison. The Zohar tells
us that when Jacob came into Egypt, this was the beginning of
the Exile. There is more commentary regarding this section than
there are verses in it because it raises so many questions. The
most significant question is the reason Jacob's journey to Egypt is
considered the beginning of the Exile. Jacob was treated royally and
given a fine tract of land where his family could reside.

The Zohar says the lesson here is that when we remove concealment
in this physical reality, as was accomplished with Joseph, the Light
of Yesod becomes revealed. We were born to undo the darkness we

have brought into this world, to remove that aspect of negativity we created in prior lifetimes. This is a procedure that happens so we can avoid the pitfalls of slavery in our own Egypt—which is the Desire for the Self Alone. Each and every form of chaos must be removed immediately before it settles. We cannot assume, once we accomplish one miracle, that we are free; we have to do it again and again.

This section brings to us the power of connections and, as we read these verses, we are developing the connection so that whatever lingers as chaos in our lives will be removed. Sometimes we have to struggle with it, even if it takes a long time. Rav Ashlag said many years ago that there is no such thing as time—time is events that pass by. When we question how long a process will take, we are subjecting ourselves to the limitations of the physical world.

8 These are the names of the sons of Israel (Jacob and his descendants) who went to Egypt: Reuben, the firstborn of Jacob. 9 The sons of Reuben: Chanoch, Pallu, Chezron, and Carmi. 10 The sons of Simeon: Yemuel, Yamin, Ohad, Yachin, Tzochar, and Shaul, the son of a Canaanite woman. 11 The sons of Levi: Gershon, Kehat, and Merari. 12 The sons of Judah: Er, Onan, Shelah, Perez, and Zerach (but Er and Onan had died in the land of Canaan). The sons of Perez: Chezron and Chamul. 13 The sons of Issachar: Tola, Fuvah, Yov, and Shimron. 14 The sons of Zevulun: Sered, Elon, and Yachle'el. 15 These were the sons Leah bore to Jacob in Paddan Aram, besides his daughter Dinah. These sons and daughters of his were thirty-three in all. 16 The sons of Gad: Tzifyon, Chaggi, Shuni, Ezbon, Eri, Arodi, and Areli. 17 The sons of Asher: Imnah, Ishvah, Ishvi, and Beriah. Their sister was Serach. The sons of Beriah: Chever and Malkiel. 18 These were the children born to Jacob by Zilpah, whom Laban had given to his daughter Leah—sixteen in all. 19 The sons of Jacob's wife Rachel: Joseph and Benjamin. 20 In Egypt, Manasseh and Ephraim were born to Joseph by Asenath, daughter of Potiphera, priest of On. 21 The sons of Benjamin: Bela, Becher, Ashbel, Gera, Naaman, Echi, Rosh, Muppim, Chuppim, and Ard. 22 These were the sons of Rachel who were born to Jacob—fourteen in all. 23 The son of Dan: Chushim. 24 The sons of Naphtali: Yachtze'el, Guni, Yetzer,

and Shillem. 25 These were the sons born to Jacob by Bilhah whom Laban had given to his daughter Rachel—seven in all. 26 All those who went to Egypt with Jacob—those who were his direct descendants, not counting his sons' wives—numbered sixty-six persons. 27 With the two sons who had been born to Joseph in Egypt, the members of Jacob's family, which went to Egypt, were seventy in all.

The Seventy Were Malchut

This section provides us with a list of how many people came to Egypt. We want to draw on their number because we know that seventy indicates Malchut, which is the all-embracing quality of this world. King David is the Chariot of Malchut, and he lived for seventy years. This section gives us the description of an entire Malchut with all the embellishments. Each person mentioned here brings with them part of the entire complement of Malchut.

These are seventy souls for the seventy nations of the world ready to transfer their energy, especially in the year when all material in the world will disintegrate. They were drawn to Egypt to transfer energy that had not been negatively affected by what was happening. These seventy souls all sold themselves to Egypt so that the children of Israel would be able to leave with all its sustenance.

28 Now Jacob sent Judah ahead of him to Joseph to get directions to Goshen. When they arrived in the region of Goshen, 29 Joseph had his chariot made ready and went to Goshen to meet his father Israel. As soon as Joseph appeared before him, he threw his arms around his father and wept for a long time. 30 Israel said to Joseph, "Now I am ready to die, since I have seen for myself that you are still alive." 31 Then Joseph said to his brothers and to his father's household, "I will go up and speak to Pharaoh and will say to him, 'My brothers and my father's household, who were living in the land of Canaan, have come to me. 32 The men are shepherds; they tend livestock, and they have brought along their flocks and herds and everything they own.' 33 When Pharaoh calls you in and asks, 'What is your occupation?' 34 you should answer, 'Your servants have tended livestock from our boyhood on, just as our fathers did.' Then you will be allowed to settle in the region of Goshen, for all shepherds are detestable to the Egyptians."

Beresheet 47:1 Joseph went and told Pharaoh, "My father and brothers, with their flocks and herds and everything they own, have come from the land of Canaan and are now in Goshen." 2 He chose five of his brothers and presented them before Pharaoh. 3 Pharaoh asked the brothers, "What is your occupation?" "Your servants are shepherds," they replied to Pharaoh, "just as our fathers were." 4 They also said to him, "We have come to live here awhile, because the famine is severe in Canaan and your servants' flocks have no pasture. So now, please let your servants settle in Goshen." 5 Pharaoh said to Joseph, "Your father and your brothers have come to you, 6 and the land of Egypt is before you; settle your father and your brothers in the best part of the land. Let them live in Goshen. And if you know of any among them with special ability, put them in charge of my own livestock." 7 Then Joseph brought his father Jacob in and presented him before Pharaoh. After Jacob blessed Pharaoh, 8 Pharaoh asked him, "How old are you?" 9 And Jacob said to Pharaoh, "The years of my pilgrimage are a hundred and thirty. My years have been few and difficult, and they do not equal the years of the pilgrimage of my fathers." 10 Then Jacob blessed Pharaoh and went out from his presence. 11 So Joseph settled his father and his brothers in Egypt and gave them property in the best part of the land, the district of Rameses, as Pharaoh directed. 12 Joseph also provided his father and his brothers and all his father's household with food, according to the number of their children. 13 There was no food, however, in the whole region because the famine was severe; both Egypt and Canaan wasted away because of the famine. 14 Joseph collected all the money that was to be found in Egypt and Canaan in payment for the grain they were buying, and he brought it to Pharaoh's palace. 15 When the money of the people of Egypt and Canaan was gone, all Egypt came to Joseph and said, "Give us food. Why should we die before your eyes? Our money is used up." 16 "Then bring your livestock," said Joseph. "I will sell you food in exchange for your livestock, since your money is gone." 17 So they brought their livestock to Joseph, and he gave them food in exchange for their horses, their sheep and goats, their cattle and donkeys. And he brought them through that year with food in exchange for all their livestock. 18 When that year was over, they came to him the following year and said, "We cannot hide from our lord the fact that since our money is gone and our livestock belongs to you, there is nothing left for our lord except our bodies and our land. 19 Why should we perish before your eyes—we and our land as well? Buy us and our land in exchange for food, and we with our land will be in bondage to Pharaoh. Give us seed so that we may live and not die, and that the land may not become desolate." 20 So Joseph bought all the land in Egypt for Pharaoh. The Egyptians, one and all, sold their fields, because the famine was too severe for them. The land became Pharaoh's, 21 and Joseph reduced the people to servitude, from one end of Egypt to the other. 22 However, he did not buy the land of the priests, because they received a regular allotment from Pharaoh and had food enough from the allotment

Pharaoh gave them. That is why they did not sell their land. 23 Joseph said to the people, "Now that I have bought you and your land today for Pharaoh, here is seed for you so you can plant the ground. 24 But when the crop comes in, give a fifth of it to Pharaoh. The other four-fifths you may keep as seed for the fields and as food for yourselves and your households and your children."

Foregoing Malchut

The matter of giving one fifth that appears in this portion is the twenty percent one is allowed to give to charity—and no more, since it is the proportion of Malchut. There are five levels of Emanation: Keter (Crown); Chochmah (Intelligence); Binah (Wisdom); Zeir Anpin (Small Face); and Malchut (Kingdom). The minute we forego Malchut, we find ourselves in Zeir Anpin.

25 "You have saved our lives," they said. "May we find favor in the eyes of our lord; we will be in bondage to Pharaoh." 26 So Joseph established it as a law concerning land in Egypt—still in force today—that a fifth of the produce belongs to Pharaoh. It was only the land of the priests that did not become Pharaoh's. 27 Now the Israelites settled in Egypt in the region of Goshen. They acquired property there and were fruitful and increased greatly in number.

Blessings from the Light

At the end of this portion, Joseph is in control of the entire world. Everyone surrendered all they had to him, their money, their land, their very lives. Joseph provided them with what they needed and could not live without. This chapter can provide us with the same.

In Genesis 27:28, it says, "The Lord shall give you of the dew of Heaven and of the fat of the earth"—and every religious person recites this. But where is this dew when we have so many problems?

Regarding the issue of entitlement—where someone feels he or she deserves something—yes it is true we are entitled to all the Light because the nature of the Light is to share. We really are entitled to everything coming to us from the Light because, more than the calf wants to suckle, the cow wants to give milk. This is the nature of the Light. Our souls came to this world for that purpose. But as far as the spirituality of the body goes, the Light does not come to us because of the principle of Bread of Shame. This is why there is a descent from the *Gimel* to the letter *Dalet*. A reduction of Light is necessary because the Light is too great, and there is pressure when we are not ready and our Vessels are too small. When there is pressure from the Light that wants to be revealed we must be very stringent and ask for more pressure. This puts pressure on the Light. If we merely ask for the Light to help us in that moment, we are living in an illusion.

Satan is clever; he appears to come from the side of the Light. This is like the person who studies all day and, when asked what he is doing, he replies, "My enemies should have to go to work, not me." He does not want to be a slave. So who is right, those who suffer with the stress and troubles of daily life or the person who does not work? Who is putting pressure on the Light?

A person has two partners—there is the Light and there is the Satan. It is difficult to get out of the cesspool that is worldly life. It is hard to change. Sometimes it seems that problems are better friends to us than happiness. Once there was a person who was very ill, and I asked him to stay for one whole Sabbath. I told him I thought he would be able to flush it out at the Kabbalah Centre but he was unable to stay. It makes no sense. When it does happen, it means there is justice. What is the problem, then? The problem is that we start to get used to the mindset of Satan, which does not allow us to see the paradox. What is the paradox? What is easy is hard; what is hard is easy; what is less is more; what is more is less.

There is a price to pay. If you want to be part of any Kabbalah Centre, you have to leave all your problems behind. Even those whose thoughts seem elevated are really operating on a lower level. Satan knows—he is listening to us right now—he even understands Hebrew. What we are doing when we scan the Zohar in Aramaic is allowing people to connect to the Light without Satan. This is the victory of the powerful being vanquished by the weak—a revolution without bloodshed, which is a miracle. It comes in a natural way, and anyone can do it. People determine this, not the Creator.

Conclusion: Not Leaving Satan a Space

There is no space between the portion of Vayigash, which is the beginning of the Exile, and the next portion, Vayechi, because we do not want to give Satan a chance—not even the slightest space to enter into. We do not wish to give him any room at all because we want to nullify him completely.

BOOK OF BERESHEET:

Portion of Vayechi

PORTION OF VAYECHI

A Summation of the Book of Beresheet

We have now come to the final section of this first book of the Bible. For those who are still unfamiliar with the significance of this scriptural tool, given not just to the Jewish people but to the entire world—as we learn both from the Talmud and in the Zohar—the Bible is an instrument with which we can radically improve our lives. Opportunities are provided each and every single week so we can alleviate some of the pain and suffering that, unfortunately, arise for many of us in unbearable and sometimes irreparable ways.

We have a unique opportunity with the reading of Vayechi because it is the final section of the first of the Five Books of Moses. It is referred to in kabbalistic terminology as Malchut—and Malchut always symbolizes the idea of the ingathering or the accumulation of all that has preceded it. From week to week, we have learned the profundity of what Creation is about; that it is not simply a fairytale, not simply something fabricated by the Bible.

The essence of the Bible solely concerns energy. It is all the technology we learn about in Kabbalah. Here, in the Kabbalah Centre, we listen to these readings in the War Room, and today such War Rooms are located at Centres all around the world. Everything we hear or read in the Bible is offered to the listener or reader, who captures the total significance of all that has transpired, beginning with the portion of Beresheet.

Some may think that if there are five Books of Moses all they have to do is hear the last portion of each book. I have to disappoint these people a little and make a distinction between listening to each week's reading of a specific book, whether it be the Book of

Beresheet or the next book, which is called the Book of Shemot—mind you do not call it Exodus—and hearing the last portion of each book. The portion read each Shabbat embraces and envelops the totality of each section; it is entirely concentrated. With Vayechi, however, we receive a drawn-out version, not as concentrated yet nevertheless still inclusive of all of the previous portions of the Book of Beresheet.

The Book of Beresheet concerns the true reality of the Tree of Life, which is why it is referred to by the word *beresheet*, which means "in the beginning." In this portion of Vayechi, all the previous portions assemble themselves to become manifest in our physical reality. We are hoping to mesh and merge the chaotic reality, which is filled with pain and suffering, with the Tree of Life Reality, so the chaos with which we are all too familiar is suddenly removed. Light and darkness cannot co-exist; one gives way to the other, and it is darkness that must recede. It is the darkness that must take a back seat, because it cannot coexist with the Lightforce of God.

We have a great opportunity here to bring the profound Lightforce of God into our physical world, the world where there is so much darkness—whether it be in the form of war, illness, poverty. We need to understand that before we connect to this reading we are in a position of power, a position where we can merge these two worlds by virtue of our consciousness.

28 Jacob lived in Egypt seventeen years, and the years of his life were a hundred and forty-seven.

Vayechi and Malchut

Being the last portion of the Book of Beresheet, Vayechi is in the frame of reference known as Malchut, which always signifies the manifestation of everything that preceded it. It can be conceived of as similar to the fruit of the tree. When a seed of that fruit is planted, the seed itself contains everything that will subsequently appear. The purpose of a seed is not for the existential beauty of the tree itself, however, but for the seed ultimately to become a fruit-bearing tree.

Malchut is the reservoir that receives all the benefits that can come to us from the Upper Levels. Everything we have read about in the previous portions of the Book of Beresheet are manifest now, and we can receive its energy as we connect with this reading.

This entire coded portion is very abstruse, as we will come to understand from the many questions raised about it by the Zohar. In fact there is very little commentary on this portion because, on the surface at least, essentially it only contains a few different aspects. What then is there to discuss? As always, we need the Zohar to reveal the Bible's true meaning.

The Ultimate Prophecy was Revealed to Jacob in the Mud

The first verse of this portion says that Jacob lived in the land of Egypt for seventeen years. The Zohar asks why we need to know that he went down to Egypt and lived there for seventeen years, when obviously we know from reading the previous portion that he was living there. The Zohar gives us a remarkable revelation: The prophecy Jacob received in Egypt—like the prophecy of Moses, who lived the crux of his life outside Israel—was of a level of consciousness that no other prophet, before or since him, has come close to achieving. Both Jacob and Moses gained a level of understanding and consciousness known as *nevu'a* (prophecy) only because they were outside the land of Israel. We know the power of the land of Israel, and we know it is called the Holy Land because it is where the spiritual center of energy is located. If Israel is where we can draw a maximum intensity of energy, then why does the Zohar conclude that *Vayechi Yaakov* or "Jacob lived," means that Jacob took all of life's existence, took the past, present, and future, from the beginning to the end—which is the *nevu'a*—and revealed it all in Egypt? The Zohar tells us the reason the Bible says "Jacob lived in Egypt" is not to reiterate that he lived in Egypt merely to fill more pages but rather it means the complete existence of life was revealed to him there.

Why would such a thing happen in Egypt? The Zohar says Egypt was the place of the first *galut* (exile), which indicates an area of the most intensely negative energy that ever existed in the world—and we know what the power of the Egyptians was and how they demonstrated that power. The Egyptians knew the art of mummification, one which has not been duplicated since. They knew how to preserve a body for thousands of years, a feat that demonstrates the Egyptians' energy-intelligence and high level of consciousness.

What is negative energy and whence does it originate? Negative energy stems from the body. The body is itself a negative energy. In fact the body knows only one kind of energy-intelligence, which is the Desire to Receive for the Self Alone. In other words, once the body partakes of food and so forth, no one else can share it since it has already been consumed by the body, and it has been centered within the body, which closes off that nourishment it receives from everyone else.

If not just the land but also the people's level of consciousness is what Egypt was about, why did the Israelites fall into captivity there? The Zohar asks if they could not have gone somewhere else. Even if Abraham had already been told by the Creator that his children would have to suffer the pain of exile, why did it happen in Egypt? Why not elsewhere? The answer is because for every positive action there is an equal and opposite negative creation of energy-intelligence—meaning everything is balanced in this world. We have choice and free will; but for every positive precept that exists in this world, there is also the force that can make us behave in a manner opposite to the consciousness of sharing and goodness.

For Jacob and Moses to achieve the level of consciousness of *nevu'a*, their revelation had to come in a place where the *botz* (mud) is located. What happens when you get stuck in the mud? The more you try to extricate yourself, the more you are unable to get out of it. It is almost as if there is a supernatural pull, a force preventing you from removing yourself. Only in Egypt could Jacob and Moses receive *nevu'a* because if the *nevu'a* had been revealed to them in Israel—in Jerusalem, where the highest intensity of positive consciousness exists—then they would not have had free choice. It would have been as if they had received a reward they did not earn.

It was an incredible accomplishment to be involved in drawing down the Light in Egypt, where negativity was so pervasive, which made it almost impossible to behave in a positive way there. Jacob and Moses were the only two people who could tolerate Egypt's 49 Gates of Negative energy, which is why everything was revealed to them there. If things come to us without difficulty, then nothing has been achieved.

Jacob and Moses attained this level of consciousness—one the Zohar says no other prophet had elevated to—because they willingly subjected themselves to an extremely negative environment. They lived in the mud, which exposed them to these negative forces. We can understand from this that if we do not go through the suffering and pain of negativity, we can never achieve the level of *vayechi*, and we will not know what it really means to "live." There is no way of measuring goodness if it is not counterbalanced by negativity. This enables us to determine what path we will choose. If someone is born into a situation of sheer positivity, their level of consciousness will not rise above the level with which they entered into this world.

How can we benefit from an understanding of this process? What does it have to do with us here and now? The answer is simple but before we discuss this answer, it is important to understand the significance and purpose of the prayer of the Berich Shemei, the prayer we recite before taking the Torah Scroll out of the Ark. The Berich Shemei comes from the Zohar and is our vehicle to bring ourselves to the point of going back in time to the revelation of the Torah on Mount Sinai where we received the Five Books of Moses, and at which point the past, present, and future all came together. In effect, we are now back in time with Jacob, back together with the energy he drew—the energy of *vayechi*, of life.

When a person becomes ill or has an accident, there seems to be absolutely no logic to it; but these things happen because we became vulnerable. If there is an empty space we do not fill with positive energy, then another energy can enter and we become vulnerable. The Zohar says that if we are not living within the frame of reference known as positivity—*Or de Chochmah* (Light of Wisdom)—we create an opening by which all forms of negativity can enter because they are always attracted to the place of lack. This is the manner in which diseases and accidents occur.

Jacob subdued, overcame, and vaporized the highest form of
negative energy—for him it became nonexistent. Therefore, when
we read the portion of Vayechi, the Zohar says that because we have
gone back in time with the Berich Shemei we are now participating
in that experience. We are there with Jacob when he draws this
energy—which he did not draw for himself but rather for all
of his family. It is said that the moment Jacob came into Egypt
the famine ceased and with his presence everything beneficent
became established because he was a *tzadik* (a righteous person).
The reason we connect with this reading is because Jacob created a
condition for all of humankind whereby negativity could no longer
become manifest.

The Benefits of Vayechi Last All Year

There is an added advantage in Vayechi not found in any other
biblical portion. Generally, the energy we can draw from the
reading on Shabbat is for six days; however, Vayechi can benefit us
for the whole year. This is because the Five Books of Moses embody
the five energy-forces. While we know there are Ten Sefirot, there
are essentially only five bottled up energies present in this world, no
more, no less—Keter, Chochmah, Binah, Zeir Anpin and Malchut.

The Book of Beresheet is called Keter, the crown and the seed.
There is one distinguishing element in the seed that makes it
different from the rest of the tree: only within the seed is contained
all that will emerge in the form of the tree, including its roots,
trunk, branches, leaves and fruit. A branch or a trunk do not
contain the tree; it is only the seed that contains all the tree's future
manifestations. Therefore, the connection formed through a reading
of the Book of Beresheet will last for the whole year because it is the
seed and includes all of the other four Books of Moses that will be

read. More importantly, the portion of Vayechi is the Malchut of Keter, the final manifestation of all that occurred before.

The Meaning of 85 Verses

It is not by chance that many are unfamiliar with the notation at the end of each chapter that marks how many verses it contains. This one in particular contains 85 verses, which makes it a very small portion compared to the others in this book. Kabbalah teaches that what is more is less, and what is less is more. Vayechi is not structured this way by chance. There is a well-defined, precise method by which the sages divided up these portions. The Bible itself does not contain divisions within each book; it only separates between one book and the next. The division of verses within each week's portion was determined by the ancient sages. Why did they decide on 85 verses for the portion of Vayechi? Why not 145 or 35? The number 85 is a clue for us.

According to the kabbalists, the Hebrew letters *Pei* and *Hei* comprise the number 85. The letters *Pei* and *Hei* spell the Hebrew word *peh*, which means "mouth," and this is the secret for the Sefira of Malchut. The mouth is the manifestation because, although we may have the thought of doing a project, unless this thought is expressed through speech to all the many people involved in it, the project cannot happen. It is the mouth that manifests the ultimate thought-consciousness; it is the vehicle by which potential becomes expressed. So with this reading we can change our physical environment.

As I have repeatedly stated, everything in the Bible is really a cosmic code. According to the Zohar, nothing is revealed with a literal superficial reading of the Bible. Rav Shimon says that he himself knew many authors who could write far better stories than those

contained in the Bible. He concludes that the superficial meaning
has no significance beyond its Zoharic interpretation, which delves
into the revelation of these codes. Rav Shimon says this portion is
completely coded because it is not directed to any of the physical
causes that create the chaos and disorder we find in our own lives.

Controlling the Mind

There are many teachers of meditation who claim that most
degenerative diseases—like heart disease, cancer and so on—are
caused by stress. Preventative medicine removes stress but it does
not remove the causes of this stress. It is understood that traumatic
conditions bring on stress; so the Zohar asks, in turn, what brought
on these traumatic conditions? Why did these conditions occur in
the first place? The Zohar concludes that the primary source does
not stem from the physical superficial level—in fact no primary
cause is located in the physical realm. If we cannot go back to the
primary source, if we cannot connect to the unseen metaphysical
cause, then there will be no true cure. We can take medicine, follow
a meditation technique, but it will be to no avail.

Take a minute, sit and try to quiet your mind. No matter what
the method, a human being can never quiet the mind by any
physical or even metaphysical technique. Why is this? According
to the Zohar, it is because everything that exists is designated by
the cosmos.

If we could take a trip to Mars or Venus and somehow control these
planets, the Zohar says we could also be in control of our lives. The
determination of illness, the determination of everything that exists
in the world, does not originate on this physical level. Everything
originates in the metaphysical realm. Who is the culprit above, the
one creating all of the havoc in the world? The Zohar says it is the

cosmos itself—but even the cosmos is not the primary source. The unseen influence of the cosmos, and its constant bombardments, will, if they remain unmanaged, in turn leave us with no control over our own lives.

The Torah Scroll was written in code because, if it related to anything of a physical nature, it could not be of any use—it could not be used as a vehicle by which we could connect to the metaphysical realm. Any form of meditation, any form of connection must relate to unseen, but nonetheless, very real forces. This is why Rav Isaac Luria's two voluminous works on the Gates of Meditation deal with the energies called Sefirot. What are Sefirot? Can we see, feel or touch them? No, they are unseen influences, and therefore, says the Zohar, if we want to take control of our lives, which is the purpose of the reading of the Torah, we must connect to the Torah on a metaphysical level. The Torah Scroll had to be written in such a way that it would not relate to anything of a physical nature—and that is the reason for the total concealment of the unseen influences it contains.

The Bible says Jacob lived in Egypt for seventeen years. The Zohar responds with an explanation that the number seventeen is a code for the word *tov*, which means "good." The Zohar provides a lengthy discussion on Jacob's ability to connect all of existence to the realm of positive energy-intelligences. The Zohar says if we wish to be in the realm of positive energy-intelligence we cannot get there by sitting down and meditating. Meditation is not, by and of itself, the means to connect with and control the planet of Saturn, which governs the month of Aquarius, the month in which this portion occurs. For that matter, it will not help with the previous month of Capricorn either, which is also governed by Saturn.

The kabbalists have provided us with one of the most powerful forms of meditation: the Ana Beko'ach, which are words of power from the Hebrew *Alef-Bet* (alphabet). The Zohar says the power of the *Alef-Bet* is the only vehicle by which we can land on the planets or reach anywhere else in the universe. How do we control such vast planetary forces? What is big is not more. The atom is extremely powerful and extremely small; fiber-optic wires are more powerful than the largest cables once used for the transmission of telephone calls. With such advances, we are moving into the Age of Aquarius, which agrees that what is less matter is better.

The Zohar says the power of the *Alef-Bet* is the only method by which we can connect to the *Vayechi Yaakov beeretz Mitzrayim* or the energy of "Jacob lived in Egypt." By not addressing the cosmic activity, we have not addressed anything. If we only address the physical problems in our bodies, we will never remove these problems. No matter how often we attempt to quiet our minds, next month, or the month after that, the stress returns. No meditation technique will ever quiet the mind permanently; not even kabbalistic meditation will quiet the mind forever. If I quiet my mind once, I have achieved the tranquility and serenity I was looking for, but only temporarily. This is why we were provided, through the Ana Beko'ach, with meditations on different Hebrew letters for each month.

The Zohar teaches that each month has its own particular bombardment of chaos that attacks us. There are two parts to every planet: the internal and the external. The external is negative and the internal is positive. If we can connect to its internal positive energy, then we have done *Vayechi Yaakov*. If we have made the *Or de Chochmah* (Light of Wisdom) manifest; we do not have to worry about the negative energy. We have already controlled the planet— we have controlled that sign of the zodiac.

The Zohar says that only by this method can we control the cosmos. Therefore, the Bible says Jacob lived in Egypt for seventeen years, since in Egypt he achieved the level of consciousness of *vayechi* because, as we have learned, seventeen is the numerical value of the word *tov* (good). We can enjoy the same beneficence as Jacob achieved when we read this chapter.

The Death of Jacob and the Responsibility of the Israelites

When the Torah Scroll is raised it can be seen that Vayechi is connected to the previous chapter. Normally there is a space between the portions with a span of five or six letters, yet here is the only place in the Torah Scroll where the gap is the space of only one letter. Most commentators, including Rashi, ask why the chapters are closed in this way. The reason is to indicate the moment that Jacob passed on (as he does later in this portion), and that the life of the Israelites was also closed down then. Because of the Israelites, all nations enjoyed prosperity and balance. Thus it stands to reason that if the Israelites do not maintain a balance amid the chaos, they become the scorn of the whole world. In truth, we are all the cause of this world's chaos and misery. Jacob, the Chariot of Tiferet, serves as a balance for the entire world—and rightly so. Rashi says this portion brought about the shutting down of life and balance, thereby invoking chaos.

There are five Books of Moses. The first one, the Book of Beresheet, is Keter, the seed. We have the opportunity with this reading— since with this Shabbat we are still at the seed level—to have the energy of Keter. There are 85 verses in this portion so that we can accumulate the energy-force of the entire book (which is Keter, seed and crown); and because the portion of Vayechi is Malchut (the physical world) of Keter it becomes one unified whole. Vayechi tells us how to live, indicating it is the chaos around us that we have no control over. If we look around at the chaos, and then measure the disunity among ourselves, it is precisely to this degree that we lack control.

What Jacob Saw, and Why he Saw it in Egypt

When the Bible says Jacob lived in the land of Egypt for seventeen years, it is telling us we can be alive but still not be *living*—we could be merely existing. What does the Bible mean when it says "Jacob lived…"? He saw through a level of prophecy called *nevu'a* that his children and descendants would live through many exiles, right up to the present time. He even saw the arrival of the Messiah (*Mashiach*). There are different levels of prophecy. When someone achieves Netzach and Hod (the levels of consciousness that exist in the Lower Triad of the Shield of David), they have achieved one level of prophecy. The Zohar further explains why Egypt was the place where Jacob acquired *nevu'a*—the level of prophecy to see the entire future. As mentioned previously, Jacob is also referred to by the name Israel. When he is Israel he is an individual who achieved his place of Tiferet in the Upper Triad, which is above the level of the Tree of Knowledge Reality. Jacob was not on the Lower Triad. He had elevated himself to the level of consciousness of the Upper Triad, where there is only the Tree of Life Reality, with no limitation of time, space or motion. In the Tree of Life Reality all the illusions of the level of the Tree of Knowledge do not exist.

The Zohar explains that *Vayechi Yaakov* (Jacob lived) is not merely to indicate that Jacob resided in Egypt. In Hebrew, the words for "he resided" are *hu gar*—and not *vayechi*. There is a distinction here, however. You could reside in a house where you sleep and eat but it does not mean you live there or even that you are really alive. You could simply exist at that address. True living is not necessarily associated with a domicile. Jacob received this level of prophecy, this high state of *nevu'a* only in Egypt.

What does the Zohar mean by prophecy? Prophecy is when one can see tomorrow, and when time, space, and motion are not limitations. Even physicists say it is all here now. Yesterday, tomorrow, and the present all exist simultaneously. Jacob's capacity for prophecy was not transient, as it never is for those who achieve the level of the Tree of Life Reality. He was on the level of the Upper Triad, where time, space, and motion cease to exist completely. Each week, on Shabbat, we achieve a connection to the Tree of Life but we can lose it the moment we think or speak about mundane matters, for example: "What should I buy today in the stock market?" Our elevated consciousness vanishes because then we are back in the Tree of Knowledge Reality. It is the unconscious part of us that is directing all our movements. For instance, when I ask myself what I should do now, a thought will come telling me what to do—yet I do not know where this thought has come from. If I go ahead and act robotically, then I am in the Tree of Knowledge Reality. When thought comes from the Tree of Life Reality, it must come without any prior thought from us.

This level of *nevu'a* exists only in the Tree of Life Reality—as it is on Shabbat when we bring our Tree of Knowledge Reality into the realm of the Tree of Life. The Zohar adds that when Jacob came to Egypt he achieved a level of prophecy that far exceeded that of all other prophecies. On previous occasions, Jacob had spoken to God himself, thereby achieving this level of prophecy. He elevated himself to a consciousness that was somewhat limited with regard to factors of time. Not only had he never achieved this level of prophecy anywhere else, but also, according to the Zohar, the level of prophecy we are discussing was not achieved by any other person besides Moses.

When Moses said he wanted to see God face to face, God's reply was: "No man looks upon My Face and lives," meaning there needs to be some form of insulation, a *masach* (curtain) between the

Lightforce and us. Otherwise the physical body would disintegrate because it cannot co-exist with the Lightforce of the Creator. Even the energy of electricity comes in an encapsulated form; a wire is insulated because direct contact with raw naked energy cannot co-exist with physicality on this level in which we find ourselves. This kind of prophecy emanates from the Light that shines of itself, as opposed to the reflective physical world, which is like the moon. It has no Light of its own, thus it cannot shine by itself. The moon can act as a channel for light but, by and of itself, it does not contain light like the sun, which has brilliance of its own and is not dependent on another celestial body to shine. When we look at the moon, we are not looking at the light of the moon. What we see is a reflection of the sun shining on the moon. This is why we say the light of the moon is a light that does not shine by and of itself.

The prophecy of Jacob came from a place like the sun, which is self-illuminated. Reflection is not as strong nor as illuminating as direct light. Almost all individuals are incapable of connecting with the Light directly. Moses and Jacob, however, were capable of connecting directly to the level of Zeir Anpin—the level that receives direct consciousness, direct thoughts, direct information, and Direct Light. This is of a much higher level of consciousness. This is how the Zohar explains the idea of *Vayechi Yaakov beeretz Mitzrayim* (And Jacob lived in Egypt). Rav Ashlag goes into a lengthy discourse on the differences between the *nevu'a* that took place in Egypt and other kinds of prophecy. When Jacob spoke to God, he had achieved a level of consciousness whereby he was in a position to draw down the Direct Light of God without fear he would disintegrate.

The Zohar says this could only have been possible in Egypt. Included within Egypt were all of the future exiles the world will endure. For when the Jewish people undergo an exile, it is not just the Jews who are punished, rather it is the entire world that suffers from a diminution or an absence of the Lightforce of God. When the Lightforce does not pervade the universe, there is darkness, and this darkness brings fragmentation and chaos.

What does the Zohar mean when it states that all of the exiles originated in Egypt? It means that all of the future exiles, including this last one, the one we currently live in, were already included in the original exile. We understand today the role played by DNA in the narrative of human evolution. When we speak of the seed we understand that all future manifestations are, on a potential level, already included within it. In this way, the future of the world already existed back there in Egypt, starting from the seed level of the first exile experienced there by the Israelites. When Jacob made this connection of deep and lasting prophecy, he was in the elevated position of *nevu'a*, and because he was not in Netzach and Hod—he was not in the Lower Triad, but the Upper Triad—consequently his *nevu'a* was not of a limited nature.

Daniel and Ezekiel had the gift of prophecy too, but their level of prophecy was limited to specific incidents only. They could not see everything from beginning to end. They were permitted vision to a certain degree. At times they also worked to achieve the consciousness to connect to Netzach and Hod, where these prophecies of a limited nature are found. When Jacob and Moses connected to the Tree of Life Reality, however, it was from the Upper Triad. Moses, as Netzach (in the Lower Triad), ultimately went up and left the realm of Malchut (our physical realm) when he left his wife and children—as we shall read in the Book of Shemot, or the Book of Names, as it should be properly translated. God called upon Moses to be completely devoted to the service of the Light. Viewed superficially, it seems cruel for God to instruct Moses to leave his wife and children, even if it is to serve the Light. Of course, God did not really send his family away. So what does it mean that Moses left his family and became completely involved in the service of God? The idea is that Moses was then connected to the realm of the Tree of Life, and that he himself became the Sefira of Daat, the connection between the Upper Three Sefirot of Keter, Chochmah, Binah and the Upper Triad of Chesed, Gevurah, Tiferet (which are Abraham, Isaac and Jacob).

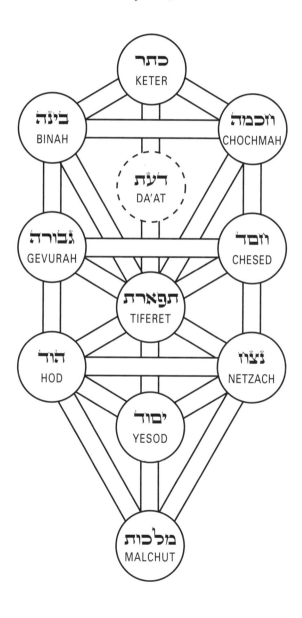

No one had achieved the same level of consciousness as Moses who was Netzach on one level of existence, and who then elevated into the area of Daat—the connection between the Upper Three Sefirot and the Upper Triad, in the realm of the Tree of Life, where illusion and chaos have no access. Daat is part of the Tree of Life, where the snake, the illusion and chaos have no access. However, the snake we call Satan can access the realm of the Upper Triad through our actions but only on certain cosmic Holy days when we have the power of connection to Chesed, Gevurah, and Tiferet.

At the time of the Morning Prayer, we are elevated into Netzach and Hod, and through our negative activities, unfortunately, we can invite the snake with us into this area of consciousness. In the area of Daat consciousness, though, Satan—that seed and composite of chaos—cannot reach us. In Daat we have a constant flow of energy; and without initiation, Daat makes the connection between the Upper Three Sefirot and the Upper Triad. Moses also achieved a connection to this level outside of Israel, where he was not subject to the influence of Satan.

As Rav Ashlag explains, the reason the Zohar says this prophecy is considered superior to a normal level of prophecy is that when Jacob was Israel he was also connected to prophecy, and he could thus foresee the future, but this was just a connection of Netzach and Hod, and therefore limited. Only in Egypt could Jacob achieve the connection to Chesed, Gevurah, and Tiferet, to a level of prophecy that was not of a limited nature. Jacob saw from beginning to end, as did Moses when he achieved an elevation to Daat (the connection between Keter, Chochmah, Binah and the lower level of consciousness) as opposed to the other prophets, like Ezekiel, Joshua, and Daniel whose vision was limited. As in an image of circles, where one penetrates the other continuously, there was a quantum effect but the quantum element was limited. Such is the nature of the levels of Netzach and Hod.

As was stated previously, Jacob achieved this kind of awareness because Egypt contained the seed of all future chaos that would ever make its appearance in the world of the Tree of Knowledge as we know it. All forms of chaos, all games that Satan would ultimately play with us, all of these future events of chaos and disorder that have ever or will ever come into our lives were all already included at the seed level in Egypt. Egypt is not just a geographical place where the Israelites would be in exile. Egypt is a totality of all the negative, chaotic consciousness that would ever make its appearance on the Earth. This is why Egypt is where the *nevu'a* of Jacob and Moses made its appearance.

This *nevu'a* could not exist in the land of Israel because Israel is one of the seven energy centers on the planet where the Lightforce is capable of being confined and harnessed, to the extent that we can make use of it. It was so with the Holy Temple in Israel; the Temple could materialize the Lightforce, even though the Lightforce is of a dimension beyond the physical reality as we know it. It is the same with the soul; a soul never requires a material aspect but becomes expressed through the blood, rather than by and of itself. Within the body, the soul finds an affinity with the blood. A soul cannot connect to the physical body but it can make its connection and create an affinity with the blood of a human being. So too, the body also finds affinity with the blood. Thus the soul and the blood have something in common and consequently, there can be communication between the two.

Jacob had achieved a level of prophecy through which he received the information about how long these exiles would be, how many there would be, and so on. We are not discussing knowing the future here, because the Zohar says it is when we devote genuine time to its study that we can really know the future. All we have to do is analyze, explore, and examine past history. Surely the past is the best teacher and the obvious foundation for the future. How could this possibly change? Consider a seed. If this year you plant an apple seed, some years from now an apple tree will emerge. Is the sapling any different in essence from the tree upon which it originated? History truly does repeat itself. Is there any reason why tomorrow would be any different from today? The future may come with different faces but we return over and over and over again to the same things. The soul does not change. The soul does not undergo any corporeality; it does not undergo materialization. The soul makes its connections by and of itself, but nothing in it undergoes any change at all.

There is nothing in the future that could not have been ascertained from previous experience. No place will undergo an ultimate devastation, such as a disastrous earthquake, unless there were prior earthquakes there of a lesser magnitude. Everything is known; there is nothing new under the sun, as King Solomon said. What the Zohar is expressing at this point about *vayechi Yaakov* is that sometimes we may have prophecy about a future event but under the weight of our other problems, we may not know how to proceed with the information.

29 When the time drew near for Israel to die, he called to his son Joseph and said to him, "If I have found favor in your eyes, put your hand under my thigh and promise that you will show me kindness and faithfulness. Do not bury me in Egypt, 30 but when I rest with my fathers, carry me out of Egypt and bury me where they are buried." "I will do as you say," he said. 31 "Swear to me," he said. Then Joseph swore to him, and Israel worshipped as he leaned on the top of his staff.

The Power of Thought

In this section, where it says "the time drew near for Israel to die, he called *to* his son Joseph and said to him..." The Zohar asks why there is a stress on the word "to." The Zohar also asks why he called only Joseph. What of his other sons? Jacob made Joseph promise to take him out of Egypt and bury him in the Cave of Machpela, where Adam and Eve, Abraham and Sarah, and Isaac and Rebecca were all buried. Why did Jacob make his son swear? Did he not trust him?

The Zohar tells us this can easily be explained. Joseph was the second-in-command of Egypt, and therefore the other brothers, who did not have such powers, may not have succeeded in taking their father from Egypt and bringing him to Hebron. Rav Shimon sees, in these few verses, another very interesting aspect and an entirely different meaning. As we know, what appears superficial to the eye or ear cannot be the real meaning. It is coded, and, as we have said, this must be so.

Rav Shimon brings up Devarim 29:29. There it says secrets belong to God, and all that is revealed belongs to us. He explains this means that one must be very careful not to go against the laws and principles of this universe because every action and every activity one performs in this world is entered into a kind of cosmic data bank. No matter what happens—even events from the most distant previous lives—these records can be retrieved. The Zohar says not only are these events registered by the individual (who sometimes forgets them), they are also registered before God, where everything is revealed. Rav Shimon says everyone should understand that all our actions are recorded and, just as it is with everything else, they too become part of the fabric of the universe.

Rav Shimon says every action—whether positive or negative—creates an equal and opposite reaction. If it is a negative activity, the result must be negative; if it is positive, the result will be positive. Whatever we think is also registered by us. The same way as an action is registered, so too, are our thoughts registered. Whether or not we pursue and manifest them, we remember everything. But what is the connection with all that Rav Shimon refers to regarding this verse? It "appears" to have no meaning. Remember, though, Jacob told Joseph to take him out of Egypt and bury him in Hebron, and he made Joseph swear. He made his son swear, as if Joseph would, for whatever reason, not want to obey his father.

The night Jacob was to marry Rachel, her father, Laban, reneged on his promise, and in her place presented Leah, the older sister. Knowing the kind of person Laban was, Jacob gave Rachel codes to present back to him on their wedding night, so he would know if it was truly Rachel or Leah. From this emerged the tradition in which we bless the bride. In essence, the blessing is also because we want to be certain ours is the designated bride. People do not know that concealing the bride is not a custom originating one thousand years ago; it is a kabbalistic practice that started with Jacob. Marriage creates one unified whole, a female with a male—Malchut with Zeir Anpin—and we cover Malchut until the marriage is consummated to concentrate on the idea that the union will take place under the *chupah*, and that up to this point there is no union.

The Zohar says for Jacob, it was Rachel with whom he was consummating the marriage. He was under the impression he was with Rachel and not Leah. This was the first time Jacob ever had intercourse, and as this was his first sperm to come forth and his thought was for Rachel, his thought-consciousness was preserved. The thought became registered; his thought of Rachel was recorded. Even though Reuben was the firstborn child born of Jacob from Leah, he presented Rachel in the place of Leah at that moment, and so Rachel's firstborn, Joseph, took the place of Reuben as the firstborn son, since it was Rachel who was with him in his energy-intelligence—which was in the form of a sperm. The Zohar briefly discusses the power of this kind of energy, and that the firstborn was Rachel's. Leah also was fully aware of what happened. She knew Jacob's thought went to Rachel and not to her.

The Zohar says the reason why the Bible stresses the word "to" in the phrase "he called *to* his son Joseph" was to indicate to us that on a physical level, Reuben was born first and yet was not considered the firstborn—his brother Joseph was. Those aspects that deal with the metaphysical consciousness are registered—they are not forgotten.

Why were people in the past not permitted to learn Kabbalah? It was said that this is because all the hidden matters in this universe belong to God, and thus we have no right to delve into them. This is not what Rav Shimon says, though. He tells us that if we do not study the hidden interpretation of the Bible then we accomplish nothing, and we walk out of life empty-handed.

If we cannot delve into the mysteries, into the metaphysical realm, how can we ever experience this beneficence that the Light wants to give us? God is not in this physical universe. He is not expressed in a physical way—and neither is thought-consciousness expressed in a physical way. Does this mean that all thought-consciousness has no validity? Does it mean that what we think means nothing? Every thought has its purpose. With the phrase "he called to his son Joseph" the secret of thought-consciousness was revealed by Joseph. Even though it was only a thought, it produced Joseph who, chronologically, was born after Reuben, yet was all the same considered to be the firstborn.

In the portion of VeZot haBracha (Devarim 33:17), when Moses discusses the blessings for all of the tribes, the Bible very clearly says Joseph was *bechor shoro*—the Bible calls him *bechor*. This was not a concoction of Rav Shimon, who never contradicts what the Bible says. What he does is to delve deeper into its real meaning because there is no answer to why it says "he called *to* his son Joseph."

The startling revelation here is that Jacob and Leah were the first to be married, yet Reuben is not considered the firstborn. This now touches on something else because, when we speak of Jacob, his overwhelming thought of what is a firstborn also prevailed over Leah's consciousness. The Bible considered only Joseph to be the firstborn, even though Reuben was the firstborn of Leah. Such is the power of Jacob's thought-consciousness. Even though, on a physical level, Joseph was not the firstborn, he was, at a higher level of consciousness, indeed the firstborn.

Rav Shimon's Prophecy

The Zohar says that in the future (after the destruction of the Holy Temple) the world will always be in crisis. The people will plead, they will yell but there will be no one listening. People all over the world will raise their heads looking for salvation, looking for ways and means whereby they can be saved—yet they will not find any form of *refu'a* (healing) or a cure for their problems and the maladies that will exist at that time.

Rav Shimon says he has found one *refu'a*. Why would there only be one? Why does the Zohar state there are no others? What did Rav Shimon foresee? It is true that Rav Shimon was a prophet; according to Rav Isaac Luria (the Ari), Rav Shimon was a reincarnation of Moses, and he, too, could see far into the future. The Ari says Rav Shimon incarnated for the express purpose of the revelation. He did not come back to this world for *tikkun*; he was a spark of Moses and was thus blessed with an integral part of Moses' soul, whereby he could see the future. Moses achieved the level of consciousness that yesterday and tomorrow merged into the present. Rav Shimon says that in the future, there will come a time when there will be but one Torah Scroll—and that this will be the only *refu'a*. When this one valid Torah Scroll is found, then all the Worlds, the Upper Worlds and the Lower Worlds, will be aroused. This goes far beyond simply possessing a valid Torah Scroll; there are conditions to this prophecy: Not only must it be a valid Torah Scroll, but the most Holy Name—*Yud*, *Hei*, *Vav*, and *Hei*, the Tetragrammaton—the most powerful demonstration in the Torah of the combination of letters, must be written in a particular way.

I must admit that until I became involved in Kabbalah I did not fully understand the importance of the ways in which the letters are written on a Torah Scroll, on the *Mezuzah* and *Tefillin*. I had no idea there were different ways the letters could be written. And if not inscribed properly these sacred instruments become invalid. According to Kabbalah, there is a difference in the way the two *Hei*'s of the Tetragrammaton are to be written. Not every Torah Scroll is written with the Tetragrammaton that is *Shem haKadosh*.

Rav Shimon says that if you have the correct kind of Torah Scroll then you have the *refu'a*; but he continues, "Woe unto those people who have a Torah Scroll that only deals with the physical superficial Illusionary Reality, and does not arouse the metaphysical cosmic consciousness." The reason I call this realm illusionary is because we have no control over it; it is elusive. You see it now, and then it disappears. We think we see things, but then they disappear. This is illusory. It is not steady, not constant—it is not eternal. The Illusionary Realm is our realm.

"Only through this authentic Torah Scroll can we arouse the metaphysical cosmic consciousness," says Rav Shimon. Therefore, wherever we pray, we should appreciate and be conscious in the knowledge that we have a Torah Scroll that can connect with and create a unification between the Upper and Lower Realms. The Zohar says it is only the power of thought that can transform a child who was not actually born first into the firstborn—and this was the thought-intelligence of Jacob.

Rav Shimon on the Senses and True Perception

Rav Shimon believes the five senses do not provide any assistance in our understanding of what is around us. The logical question then is: why do we have them? Are they here simply to confuse us? We know the eyes and the ears do not always see and hear correctly. The Zohar says the five senses can never ever be put to use for obtaining clarity or understanding. Does the Lord, whose intrinsic characteristic is to share, want to destroy the world? If that is so, why did He create it in the first place? The Lord does not want to destroy the world; He wants to benefit the world—which is the sole reason He created it. The Zohar uses the expression "the intention of the Lord falls on deaf ears, and blind eyes." The Zohar says that through the Bible we can achieve a level of consciousness beyond the awareness of what the eye sees and the ear hears. The senses are instruments that can be useful if they are used properly—for example, when the ear hears the Torah reading on Shabbat. Without hearing the words, we would not be in a position to connect with that which is read. Thus we can comprehend that the ears and eyes have a purpose. However, Rav Shimon tells us they only act as channels, and are never to be considered the support mechanisms to make use of in achieving a greater understanding of any given situation. Our eyes and ears are closed to understanding and to any true awareness of what goes on around us. This is why Vayechi stands out as one of those portions of exceptional importance to assist us.

Beresheet 48:1 Some time later Joseph was told, "Your father is ill." So he took his two sons Manasseh and Ephraim along with him. 2 When Jacob was told, "Your son Joseph has come to you," Israel rallied his strength and sat up on the bed. 3 Jacob said to Joseph, "God Almighty appeared to me at Luz in the land of Canaan, and there He blessed me, 4 and said to me, 'I am going to make you fruitful and will increase your numbers. I will make you a community of peoples, and I will give this land as an everlasting possession to your descendants after you.' 5 Now then, your two sons born to you in Egypt before I came to you here will be reckoned as mine; Ephraim and Manasseh will be mine, just as Reuben and Simeon are mine. 6 Any children born to you after them will be yours; in the territory they inherit they will be reckoned under the names of their brothers.

Learning from Jacob How to Take Control

The Zohar says when we hear the words *avicha chola* (your father is ill), we generally associate this with difficult times and not with Jacob, and it will enter into the realm of the unconscious—this is the power of Satan. When we do this, we become entangled with the sickness of the world. This is where the idea of a little knowledge being a dangerous thing enters into it. We believe what we know exists, and that what we do not know does not exist. Why do we exist? Is it because enlightenment philosophy says "I think therefore I am."? Logicians say if one does not see the chair, then the chair does not exist. The person who reads the words *avicha chola* and associates it with difficult times is already connected to the physical reality of chaos and disorder.

However, we can say, "I am going to control the knowledge of non-existence," as Jacob did in Egypt. With the blessings Jacob gave to his sons, he gave us control over the future—control over Satan. We have to take Satan by the tail and say, "I'm going to control you." If there is no Satan to control, there is no complete control at all. Jacob and Moses had to be in Egypt to take control of Satan because that is his habitat. It is not only his but it is also the habitat of all future agents of Satan—Egypt contains all of the future chaos that is yet to come. Hence we should know what avicha chole means and we should not connect to it. Of course—beware!—there is a danger here. When Jacob wrestled with the angel, he got dirty. If you play in the mud you will get dirty; it is inevitable.

Satan came to God and asked Him to get rid of Rav Shimon Bar Yochai. He requested this because wherever he hid, Rav Shimon sought him out and took control over him. Satan wanted to know, under these conditions, what his purpose is on Earth. Such is the level of consciousness of Rav Shimon. There was nothing he could not control. This is what Jacob and Moses needed; this is *vayechi* (and he lived).

The lesson of Vayechi is not that we should run to a mountain retreat to meditate and relax. Even there, we would have memories of the very troubles we ran from. The only place where we can make our troubles disappear is in the mud. Every single person can be a ruler. However, only after we have been through the mud can we become a true leader; only then can we rule with wisdom. Only when we are in the mud can true achievements be made. Chaos does not disappear because we have taken a vacation. We must maintain constant control.

Why Jacob Chose Two Grandchildren Born in Egypt

When Joseph was told his father was ill, he took his two sons, Manasseh and Ephraim to see Jacob. Jacob said that these two sons of Joseph, born in Egypt, would now be considered as his own. Manasseh and Ephraim would replace Joseph and the tribe of Levi—with regard to the division of the land of Israel—once the Israelites entered and captured the land with Joshua. Since both Manasseh and Ephraim participated in the division of the land, it meant that Joseph in effect received two portions. From what has been said up to this part of the story, we now know Joseph was the true firstborn and as such, he was entitled to two portions of the land. If he was not the firstborn, why would Jacob have chosen both Manasseh and Ephraim?

Why did Jacob single out these two grandchildren and say they would become part of the twelve tribes, replacing the tribes of Levi and Joseph? The reason they were chosen is because these two were born in Egypt before Jacob came there. The Zohar says Israel (Jacob) was in the Upper Realm and could not be touched by Satan. Satan finds no home in anyone who has reached the Tree of Life Reality.

This portion is not here to tell us about the greatness of Israel (Jacob) and the upper elevations to which he and Moses transcended. It does not exist to provide us with a recording of history. It is here for us, to show us that these two grandsons would be included as part of the twelve tribes because they were born in the mud—because they were born where Satan originated. Without the Zohar, we would not be aware that such opportunities exist.

How do we extricate ourselves from a problem? Who does not want financial security? Who does not want to be free from illness? This reading can provide such security and freedom. But Rav Shimon says those who do not have the merit cannot show up to the Torah reading on Shabbat. The opportunity is there but it does not mean every one of us will always be able to take advantage of it. The Torah, given on Mount Sinai, has the power to purify and eliminate the world of the Tree of Knowledge. But that does not necessarily mean Satan cannot put a few stumbling blocks along the way to prevent us from making the connection—even to the point that there will be someone who reads the verse "Jacob became ill," and says, "Oh dear, the poor fellow got sick." This way of thinking dissipates any energy that would have been acquired because the connection was made, in this case, only to illness.

The Zohar says the reason the Bible states that Jacob was ill is to tell us to take illness by the tail and control it. This verse does not indicate that the patriarch was literally unwell. We cannot become caught up in a superficial interpretation, for then we have lost the consciousness of control. It is much like someone drowning in business troubles. Do they try listening to new ideas? The troubled individual is so wrapped up in their petty concerns that they cannot listen to the person trying to tell them they have the solution needed to correct these troubles. Very few people in this type of situation will listen to the right answer.

The Zohar says this portion is providing us with an opportunity that comes once a year, to leap over the scripts of our own individual lives. These two sons were born outside of Israel among the nations of the world (the exiles), and therefore born outside of protection. From this point on, however, they were considered to be within the confines of Jacob's protection. When people read this section, many believe Jacob favored these two grandchildren and that this favoritism is why he chose them to be his own two sons— but it is not so. He chose them because they were born with Satan and had the seed of exile in them.

We are not dealing here with physical places that are good or evil. One could be in Israel and be inundated with problems; the physical land is not what determines the nature of freedom or chaos. This portion is about the removal of the dominion of Satan over our lives. By his action, Jacob brought Satan into the realm of his control.

7 As I was returning from Paddan, to my sorrow Rachel died in the land of Canaan while we were still on the way, a little distance from Ephrath. So I buried her there beside the road to Ephrath that is, Bethlehem." 8 When Israel saw the sons of Joseph, he asked, "Who are these?"

The Stories in the Torah are a Mirror Held up to Our Own Lives

In Beresheet 48:8, Jacob asked who these children were, as though he had not just acknowledged they were Joseph's sons. Rashi comments that this is because they were not worthy of the blessing. As we have explained on many occasions, the Bible is really a secret code that cannot in any way be understood literally. The stories of Joseph's life are unbelievable. The sale of Joseph by his brothers, for example; or Joseph not informing his father he was alive; or instructing his brothers to bring Benjamin, knowing it would be painful to his father to have the second son of his beloved Rachel taken away. None of these events make sense unless we consider the Zoharic interpretation, which says that these people are actually a portrayal of our own insanity. How many times have we—for all of the "good" reasons—betrayed the trust of those who have placed their confidence in us? So often when someone does something good for us, all of a sudden we do not know them anymore. We ought never to forget what someone has done for us, no matter how insignificant or how long ago it was. There is never justification for treating another person with anything less than human dignity. Limiting oneself to certain foods or acting more holy outwardly does not mean we are righteous. Anyone who intentionally hurts others, even in the name of justice or righteousness, is wrong.

Through his actions, Jacob suggests these two sons of Joseph were deserving of a blessing. But then he reconsidered, thinking they were not ready. In the end Jacob blessed them anyway. His actions were a reflection of humankind, we who have not yet learned that there are universal laws. The Jews were entrusted with this concept to bring it to the world but instead they brought Christianity and Islam to further confuse the truth. God does not need us to be righteous, holy or religious. In this world there are universal laws; if people have a desire to listen they can—but they are not obliged to do it. However, everyone should know that the consequences of violating universal laws are inevitable.

Satan prefers to hear from us that we believe there are no duties in this world, that we have no responsibility to others. Responsibility towards others is a universal law because the universe is unified. We cannot ignore our fingers if we accidentally place them on a burning stove.

To the extent we can think of others, that is the extent to which we are like God. Every day, I get so many of calls from people pleading, "Help me!" or "Save me!" I want to say, "You don't need me; you are like God. Does God have to ask for help? Why then do you need someone else to help you?" This is a difficult concept to entertain, and I understand why. It is because so many millennia have passed with a fixed consciousness that we must pray to God to help us.

9 "They are the sons God has given me here," Joseph said to his father. Then Israel said, "Bring them to me so I may bless them." 10 Now Israel's eyes were failing because of old age, and he could hardly see. So Joseph brought his sons close to him, and his father kissed them and embraced them. 11 Israel said to Joseph, "I never expected to see your face again, and now God has allowed me to see your children too." 12 Then Joseph removed them from Israel's knees and bowed down with his face to the ground. 13 And Joseph took both of them, Ephraim on his right toward Israel's left hand and Manasseh on his left toward Israel's right hand, and brought them close to him. 14 But Israel reached out his right hand and put it on Ephraim's head, though he was the younger, and crossing his arms, he put his left hand on Manasseh's head, even though Manasseh was the firstborn. 15 Then he blessed Joseph and said, "May the God before whom my fathers Abraham and Isaac walked, the God who has been my shepherd all my life to this day, 16 the Angel who has delivered me from all harm—may he bless these boys. May they be called by my name and the names of my fathers Abraham and Isaac, and may they increase greatly upon the earth." 17 When Joseph saw his father placing his right hand on Ephraim's head he was displeased; so he took hold of his father's hand to move it from Ephraim's head to Manasseh's head. 18 Joseph said to him, "No, my father, this

one is the firstborn; put your right hand on his head." 19 But his father refused and said, "I know, my son, I know. He too will become a people, and he too will become great. Nevertheless, his younger brother will be greater than he, and his descendants will become a group of nations." 20 He blessed them that day and said, "In your name will Israel pronounce this blessing: 'May God make you like Ephraim and Manasseh.' " So he put Ephraim ahead of Manasseh. 21 Then Israel said to Joseph, "I am about to die, but God will be with you and take you back to the land of your fathers. 22 And to you, as one who is over your brothers, I give the ridge of land I took from the Amorites with my sword and my bow."

Jacob's Blessing

Jacob placed his right hand on Ephraim and his left hand on Manasseh. Even though his right hand should have been placed on Manasseh, who was the elder of the two sons of Joseph, and his left hand on Ephraim, the younger. What is the meaning of this? The twelve tribes were established with the twelve sons of Jacob, as were the twelve signs of the zodiac. Manasseh and Ephraim were put in the place of two other sons, Levi and Reuben.

A blessing consists of a sequence of letters, which provide us with the removal of chaos. We recite the Ana Beko'ach meditation three times a day because we know the totality is in the seed from whence it comes.

What would the other children and grandchildren say regarding this blessing? Was Jacob favoring Joseph again? For the kabbalist this is not even a question. Why? Because everything can be changed. Wherever chaos exists it does not belong and can be eradicated. Satan wants us to believe we cannot change chaos, that chaos is too well established. It is always the body that requires things the soul does not need.

The idea is to be in control of things before they manifest. Once you are stuck in the mud it is difficult to get out. Jacob is not blessing his children in any conventional way. To the kabbalist, a blessing means receiving a sequence of letters that can prevent negative energy from being channeled by a celestial body.

Why Jacob Gave the Younger Son the Firstborn Blessing

The Bible says Jacob's eyes became heavy with age and he could not see well. He asked that Joseph bring his grandchildren closer to him so he could bless them. To receive the blessing Joseph put Ephraim on the left side of Jacob, since he was the younger child, and Manasseh on Jacob's right. The Bible says Israel crossed and extended his right hand and put it on the younger son and his left hand he placed on Manasseh, the older son. If Jacob's eyes were heavy with age, how was he aware enough to switch his hands? Even Joseph was under the impression his father might be confused because he tried to move Jacob's hands, putting them in the "proper" position.

But Jacob knew what he was doing. He saw into the future. The Zohar explains that the eyes do not truly see. The Bible wants to tell us that just as Jacob was blind in the physical world, so are we blind who do not see the Light. Jacob knew who the true firstborn was because he had achieved another level of consciousness. The eyes are not what allow a person to see. What allows a person to see is his connection. Who was firstborn is a matter of thought-consciousness; the younger son achieved a certain level of consciousness that allowed him to be the true firstborn. Jacob knew Manasseh would bring idol-worship back into the Temple. And because of the knowledge of where this line of the family was going, he did not want to inject the line of Manasseh with the energy of the firstborn blessing.

The Zohar asks if Jacob really blessed the sons of Joseph. The Bible says he blessed Joseph. Jacob wanted to bless the two children—with the same blessing that fathers still bless their children (until the age of twenty) every Friday night. So the Zohar asks why the Bible says Jacob blessed Joseph without telling us how he blessed him. It just says "he blessed Joseph." Why should Jacob single Joseph out once again as the favored child—as he did before, by making him a beautiful garment?

Then the Bible tells us that Jacob says, "the Angel who has delivered me from all harm—may he bless these boys. May they be called by my name and the names of my fathers, Abraham and Isaac, and may they increase greatly upon the earth." Why did he not choose any of the other grandchildren? Why did Jacob stress the fact that they were born before he arrived to Egypt? Jacob also added that none of the other children born of Joseph would be included in the division of the two portions of land—only these two sons.

A blessing is thought-intelligence, a transfer of energy. It is the same when the Kohanim (priests) perform their blessing. They act as a channel for the energy of the Lightforce. A Kohan is the proper vessel, one who acts as a channel to transfer the metaphysical energy of the Lightforce of the Creator—energy that will continue on and on, unlike a battery or electricity that comes to an end. It is not a blessing for today only. It is a blessing where a certain amount of energy is captured and will continue on through the channel of a knowledgeable Kohan. From his prior experience, Jacob understood thought-consciousness. He knew his blessing would travel in the same way as his thought-consciousness traveled until the moment Joseph was born as the true firstborn. This is the power of energy; this is the power of the blessings of Jacob that take place in this portion.

There are 85 verses in the portion—the manifestation of power. A blessing without the appropriate meditation to channel energy is simply a few nice words. When a father blesses his children and feels he can act as a channel for them, this is a blessing indeed. Blessing means the transfer of a force of energy that is called *Or deChochmah* (Light of Wisdom).

The Zohar explains that when the Bible says Jacob blessed Joseph, the Bible does not detail this blessing as it does with the individual blessings given to the other children. The blessing Jacob extended to the sons of Joseph also included a blessing for Joseph. The Zohar asks why Jacob stressed the blessing of the children. And then the Zohar answers this with something a little strange: a grandfather loves his grandchildren more than he loves his children. Why? We know that, on a strictly physical level, grandfathers often have more time to give attention to their grandchildren than they did with their own children in their younger days. Is this what the Zohar is referring to? The Zohar says when Jacob blessed the children there was a transfer of energy, and that Jacob was, in essence, using Joseph. It does not say he blessed the children, rather he blessed Joseph, and through Joseph the blessing included the children.

Sometimes people ask for a blessing to be directed towards their business or some other problem. However, do we really want to limit a blessing? Do we want to limit the extent of the channel and energy to one area alone? People do not fully understand what it means to receive a blessing. A blessing refers to the Lightforce of the Creator, and that energy is all pervasive—it should travel wherever it is meant to travel without being directed. Jacob was so careful that, although he was blind, he knew the energy of a blessing travels far and wide. His blindness did not inhibit him from achieving a higher level of consciousness because, according to the Zohar, everyone is blind. Whoever uses their eyes alone to perceive the nature of reality is blind.

Jacob was physically blind, so the question remains this: Without sight, how did he know to switch his hands? How do we come to know people? Is it because we see them physically or do we receive a vibration about them and know exactly what they are about? If a man dresses in a nice suit or drives a Jaguar, do those things make him a decent person? And if he drives an old jalopy does this mean is he not such a nice person? Is this all the eye can do for us?

The reason this portion is so important is because the blessing each tribe received was a connection to every sign of the zodiac. When we listen to or read this portion we are receiving a connection to the positive aspect of the cosmos. Each sign of the zodiac contains both positive and negative energy-intelligences, and both of these intelligences have influence.

These blessings, like the Ana Beko'ach, cover the individual and do not allow in any vulnerability. They do not permit a space by which the negative energy can continually bombard us. The Zohar says that when one is born under a certain zodiacal sign, this is what you are. We can take advantage of the positive energy that comes out of this month, or the negative energy—because we have free will.

The blessings Jacob gave are meant to enable us to overcome all of the negative energy-intelligences of any particular month. If we do not create what I call, a "security shield" then we are vulnerable to the negative influences that bombard us day and night—the cosmos does not sleep. For some people, thousands of thoughts come in when they are trying to fall asleep at night. Where do these thoughts come from? Can we quiet the mind when we make a conscious effort to do so? Never! We are powerless to control the mind. The only thing we can do with the mind is to use the proper channels to draw down the blessing of the particular month we are experiencing. If we are surrounded with positive energy, we have created a security shield, and the daily bombardment will not affect us.

This, the Zohar says, is the power of thought. If we do not have this power of thought or we do not inject the power of thought into our lives, then we have accomplished nothing. We are blind. The Zohar says if we consider the mind as the primary source of everything we do, and it is upon the mind that all of our success or failure depends, then we are vulnerable to all of the negative energy-intelligences around us. In thinking that everything originates in the mind, that the mind is the primary source, then we have permitted a vulnerability to exist.

A blessing is the words by which we receive the direct connection to the Tree of Life Reality. A blessing represents a sequence of letters that does away with chaos.

Exile, Redemption and Quantum Leaps through Personal Destiny

The Zohar says the verse that describes Jacob's blessing to Joseph and his children is not here to let us know what happened with Joseph and his children. Rather it is meant to enlighten us about what will take place in the future. Was it unfair that Jacob called Joseph to bless him and his two sons privately? The Zohar, written

2,000 years ago, says it was not unfair. Joseph is the sixth Sefira (Yesod), and the ultimate redemption will come at the end of 6,000 years, which is an indication of the exile's length. What does exile mean? How are we to understand it? After all, not everyone is in exile. Many people living in the United States do not feel they are living in exile; to them the United States is freedom, and those who have freedom have all the blessings that can be bestowed upon them. People who live in Israel do not feel they are in exile either. So what are we to understand from the idea of exile?

The concept of exile or redemption is not referring to a nation but rather it is an individual experience—we are either connected to the Tree of Life or we are in exile. To be connected to the Tree of Life is to be redeemed. What does it mean to be redeemed? Those who have been redeemed have been taken out, they have been released, liberated, freed. In the case of the precept known as the Redemption of the Firstborn, we take the child out of the realm of death and bring him into the realm of life. Redemption is not some religious notion of being rescued by God. To redeem is to move out from exile. The word "redemption" means there is an exchange of something in the present for something better in the future.

When we read this section on Shabbat, this event brings us to the end of 6,000 years. If we have the consciousness, we have an opportunity to bypass all of the physical events that have already been included in our personal narrative—those physical events that we must go through because of the necessary cleansing processes from prior incarnations or for some evildoing we may have engaged in during this present lifetime. All of these necessary cleansings are called a period of exile. It is the period where there is no control over the events of the Tree of Knowledge Reality, over the events of havoc, disaster, and incessant trouble. What Joseph did here was to create a quantum leap right to the end, where there is always a good conclusion. What is the end? Does it mean that when a person reaches 98 or 120 years of age things will be good for them? Not necessarily, because for some the end might be another incarnation, so it is an ongoing process of cleansing.

Being certain that at the end things will be good, however, is a cardinal rule. When someone has completed all of their purification, they come to a place where there is no chaos, and none of the individual misfortunes each one us has been afflicted with, exist. With Kabbalah, though, we learn that we can take a quantum leap and skip right over those events in our narrative that we must otherwise all weave our way through.

By connecting to this blessing for Joseph, we have an opportunity to make a giant leap over the events of tomorrow and the next day, if they spell out disaster. Disaster and chaos are within the realms of illusory time. When an individual goes bankrupt, does it mean they are finished? Not necessarily; and not everyone who becomes ill dies of their sickness; not everyone who experiences marital or domestic problems comes to the end of happiness. These painful experiences may just be stages the individual goes through to arrive at an ultimate place in life called happiness.

This story is talking about making a quantum leap—and we can speed up this process. The trouble is that for too many thousands of years our minds have been placed in the back seat. We have not made use of our minds. The reason why we have this story and the blessing of the ultimate redemption is so we can take a giant leap right into the last moment, the moment when the world of illusion, uncertainty and chaos comes to an end.

Beresheet 49:1 Then Jacob called for his sons and said: "Gather around so I can tell you what will happen to you in days to come. 2 Assemble and listen, sons of Jacob; listen to your father Israel.

Jacob, His Prophecies and Blessings

In the portion of Vayechi, Jacob wants to provide us with the means for living. We may have prophecy of a limited nature to know what we should be doing tomorrow but this does not necessarily mean we are in a better position. What about the unforeseen circumstances we may not have access to? Remember, prophecy can provide us with some information in Netzach and Hod but this is of a limited nature. For example, while a person may see how they might easily make a fortune, they may nonetheless suffer a heart attack before this future financial security begins—then what is the good of it all?

Previously, we asked the question of why Jacob and Moses received *nevu'a* in Egypt. Why could they not receive the same prophecy in Israel, where the levels of consciousness were much higher in nature? The answer is that knowing what the future will be is different from controlling it. These are two different aspects of the same thing. What both Jacob and Moses understood was that if you want to control all future events you must deal with the chaos—you must deal with Malchut.

Vayechi, the last portion of the Book of Beresheet, is Malchut because it is an accumulation of all the energies that have been captured each week since the first portion of the book was read.

As stated previously, there are 85 verses in Vayechi. The number 85 is the numerical value of the word *peh*, which means "mouth" or "expression." The mouth is also the level of Malchut. The head contains the five Sefirot: Keter is the brain, the eyes are Chochmah, the ears are Binah, and the nose is Zeir Anpin, while the mouth represents the level of consciousness of Malchut, the material world. The sages provide us with a clue here: Both Jacob and Moses understood that if you want to control all future events you must deal with the chaos, you must deal with the Malchut. The culmination, the realization, and the materialization all exist in Malchut. What Jacob provided for us here in this section, as well as throughout the portion of Vayechi, is the understanding that it is not enough to know what the future will be—we can also control the events that will be forthcoming.

Isaiah and Jeremiah predicted that the end of the Holy Temple was drawing close, and they pleaded with the people to change their ways so its destruction would not come to pass. But the people did not listen. In this chapter, not only did Jacob receive the prophecy of all the future exiles that would take place, he also learned what could be done about it. He learned how and when these exiles could be prevented from taking their prescribed course. According to the Zohar, Vayechi contains the power we can receive, in the world of Malchut, to deal with every exile that would ultimately make its appearance. This chance comes every year, and if we are aware of it, all the future events on this level of existence can be foretold.

In this portion we learn how we can eliminate the Tree of Knowledge Reality. Would that be a miracle? No, because miracles only exist on this physical level, where we have no control over the Tree of Knowledge Reality. God did not create misfortune; the Tree of Life Reality never undergoes changes. The only changes we can observe are in the physical reality. A child is born, becomes a young woman, and then she gets older. What gets older—her soul? Do we celebrate the soul's birthday each year? No, we celebrate the body's birthday. The soul does not undergo change but coexists together with the physical body. Since we have not achieved that level of consciousness whereby we are constantly in touch with the Tree of Life Reality, we experience chaos and aging. The fact that chaos can be washed out in an instant is a rarity of our human condition. But when we look around, it seems as if there are more sick people than healthy ones; and everyone ultimately falls into illness, financial insecurity, and so on. The prophecies of Jacob and Moses dealt with the realm of the Tree of Knowledge because only from that realm can we make changes.

Unless a *tzadik* (righteous person) attains the level of the Tree of Life Reality, he or she would never overcome problems of the Tree of Knowledge Reality. This is why Jacob had to flee his brother Esau, and for years work for and be tricked by his wicked uncle, Laban. This is also why he had to suffer the disappearance of his beloved son, Joseph, whom he presumed to be dead. Moses, too, had to overcome the problems of this physical dimension. He was raised apart from his true family; then he encountered strife with the Pharaoh and conflict with his own people, after saving them from their slavery. The lives of these patriarchs were not those of contentment and serenity. They were always facing problems. Why did they undergo such chaos? The answer is that it was for our benefit. Each time we read in the Bible about an incident where they overcame problems of the Tree of Knowledge Reality, this is our opportunity to overtake the chaos and havoc we see around us.

We are in a position of overcoming whatever insecurities and uncertainties that are in store in the future. The reason this *nevu'a* took place in Egypt, and not in Israel, was to allow us to overcome, master and have dominion over the world of the Tree of Knowledge, with all of its chaos—this is the level of reality that has to be dealt with. That was why Moses fled Pharaoh and came back only to experience forty of the most difficult years, along with constant trouble from the Israelites he led. Only in the realm of the Tree of Knowledge could Moses provide for us in the future the opportunity to overcome as he overcame—and he was not subject to such rules as we are. This prophecy was not merely to predict what was to come but also what can be done about it. In Vayechi, Jacob not only received the prophecy of all the future exiles that would take place, but he also learned what could be done about them.

The Bible says clearly that when Jacob assembled the children he said to all of them, "Gather around, I want to tell you everything that will ever take place in the days to come. Gather and listen to my words. Listen to the words of Israel, your father." What exactly happened here? He blessed each son, without telling them what would occur in the future. Did Jacob contradict himself?

According to the Zohar, it makes no difference what the future has in store. This reading is giving us a remedy by which to change it all. What Jacob achieved when he blessed his sons is a blessing in disguise. But not in the sense that we normally understand this expression to mean. Rather the blessing is disguised in every single word. There is no mention here that Jacob was going to bless his children but when you read it, you know what he achieved here. Sometimes it does not seem to be a blessing.

Jacob cursed the anger of Simeon and Levi, yet it is always translated to mean he gave them a blessing. We should remember Simeon and Levi destroyed the entire city of Shechem and murdered all the male population of Nablus. But he did not gather his sons to give them a blessing—the Bible does not say that. In the absence of the Zohar, how else would one translate this? What is the connection? The remedy for today until the end of our days is right here in this section. We can take these quantum leaps and cut out much of our narrative and bring tomorrow, or 227 years hence, here today.

All the previous portions provide us with tools each and every single week as we read the Bible, while at the same time refreshing our memory and raising our consciousness to understand what is really happening all around us. Unfortunately, most of us are groping in the dark. Whether in the realms of science, politics, medicine and so on, chaos, regrettably, seems to reign supreme.

One of the strangest aspects of this reading is that Jacob said he would reveal all that would take place throughout the generations up until the end of time, by removing the veil we call yesterday, today, and tomorrow—and by opening up the whole of the universe. Yet nowhere in the verses that follow is there a prophetic revelation of any sort. Did we expect Jacob to burden us with a trillion volumes to record everything that would take place everywhere over the coming millennia?

The Zohar explains that the blessings are actually secrets of the last days. The word blessing, as we have come to understand it, is the transference of the Lightforce of God controlled and channeled into this chaotic reality. With this reading we have the opportunity to capture and instill within ourselves all the Light not only within this month but also during all twelve months of the year.

In Beresheet 48:16, we have a collection of words we have now come to understand are not merely a blessing but rather they represent a universal channel not limited to any one sector of humanity, not limited to any one race or one religion. This blessing of Jacob encapsulates the totality of the Lightforce as a bestowing agent, transformer, and transmitter of the Lightforce of God. The intent of Jacob was to tell us that in the absence of the Light, chaos comes in unlimited ways. Yet there is a solution to the infinite pain and suffering that will be endured over time. According to the kabbalist, the singular cause of the countless varieties of chaos, the woes that afflict humankind, is the absence of Light.

As a Chariot of Tiferet, Jacob is connected to the Tree of Life Reality. And these blessings were a transferal of the Lightforce of God from Jacob—this is the power he was given to empower us. With these blessings, chaos as we know it—even though it may appear to be totally irrevocable—will disappear. While chaos may reign supreme in our minds, once we have made our connections and used the kabbalistic tools and disciplines available to us, there is no question that we can draw into ourselves the awesome power known as the Lightforce of God, and thereby completely eliminate chaotic influences regardless of time, space, and motion. Then we will be able to send energy thousands of miles away to people in need of Light, transferring to them healing energies and the Lightforce of God. We have come upon the dawning of a new era.

3 "Reuben, you are my firstborn, my might, the first sign of my strength, excelling in honor, excelling in power. 4 Turbulent as the waters, you will no longer excel, for you went up onto your father's bed, onto my couch and defiled it. 5 Simeon and Levi are brothers—their swords are weapons of violence. 6 Let me not enter their council, let me not join their assembly, for they have killed men in their anger and hamstrung oxen as they pleased. 7 Cursed be their anger, so fierce, and their fury, so cruel! I will scatter them in Jacob and disperse them in Israel. 8 Judah, your brothers will praise you; your hand will be on the neck of your enemies; your father's sons will bow down to you. 9 You are a lion's cub, Judah; you return from the prey, my son. Like a lion he crouches and lies down, like a lioness—who dares to rouse him? 10 The scepter will not depart from Judah; nor the ruler's staff from between his feet, until he comes to whom it belongs and the obedience of the nations is his. 11 He will tether his donkey to a vine, his colt to the choicest branch; he will wash his garments in wine, his robes in the blood of grapes. 12 His eyes will be darker than wine, his teeth whiter than milk.

The Blessing of Judah and Mashiach

We read in Genesis 49:8 about the blessing of Yehuda (Judah), who corresponds to the month and zodiac sign of Cancer. Usually in the Torah Scroll there is a letter *Vav* at the top of each column, which represents balance. In verse 8, Yehuda's name is on the top of the column, so the letter Yud is at the beginning, not a *Vav*. Why here and why with the name of Yehuda? It also says *Yehuda atah*. Nowhere else does the Torah Scroll refer to someone as *atah*. Yehuda represents the Messiah (*Mashiach*)—*Mashiach ben David*. King David originated from the tribe of Yehuda. When there is chaos, there is no *Mashiach*, when there is *Mashiach* there is no chaos; they cannot co-exist.

You may ask why *Mashiach* has not yet arrived. There are a few possible times in history where *Mashiach* could have come. In the time of Rav Isaac Luria (the Ari), he told his students one Shabbat that they have the opportunity to bring *Mashiach*. The only condition was that they needed to have unity. Everything was going well until the Third Meal, when two children started to fight and the parents got involved.

We say we do not want chaos, so why do we not change? It would seem that we want chaos. Therefore, we have exactly what we want. What we do not want, we do not have. Satan wants us to look around and see nothing but problems. He is very strong, making us think we see chaos. But where does the chaos come from? It is caused only by our own negative actions. More important than sharing is restriction of negative actions.

All the blessings for the sons were very brief, except when it came to Yehuda, who governs the month of Cancer. Jacob knew that in the last days of the world the ultimate power of destruction would be the power of cancer. This is rooted in the cancerous thoughts within us. There is no cure, and science will not find one. Only through the power of Kabbalah can we remove it.

13 Zebulun will live by the seashore and become a haven for ships; his border will extend toward Sidon. 14 Issachar is a rawboned donkey lying down between two saddlebags. 15 When he sees how good is his resting place and how pleasant is his land, he will bend his shoulder to the burden and submit to forced labor. 16 Dan will provide justice for his people as one of the tribes of Israel. 17 Dan will be a serpent by the roadside, a viper along the path that bites the horse's heels so that its rider tumbles backward. 18 I look for your deliverance, O Lord. 19 Gad will be attacked by a band of raiders, but he will attack them at their heels. 20 Asher's food will be rich; he will provide delicacies fit for a king. 21 Naphtali is a doe set free that bears beautiful fawns. 22 Joseph is a fruitful vine, a fruitful vine near a spring, whose branches climb over a wall. 23 With bitterness, archers attacked him; they shot at him with hostility, 24 but his bow remained steady, his strong arms stayed limber, because of the hand of the Mighty One of Jacob, because of the Shepherd, the Rock of Israel, 25 because of your father's God, who helps you, because of the Almighty, who blesses you with blessings of the heavens above, blessings of the deep that lies below, blessings of the breast and womb. 26 Your father's blessings are greater than the blessings of the ancient mountains, than the bounty of the age-old hills. Let all these rest on the head of Joseph, on the brow of the prince among his brothers.

27 Benjamin is a ravenous wolf; in the morning he devours the prey, in the evening he divides the plunder." 28 All these are the twelve tribes of Israel, and this is what their father said to them when he blessed them, giving each the blessing appropriate to him.

Predictions and Troubles

Jacob blessed the children but nowhere is there any mention of what was going to happen to them. The Midrash says the Shechinah left Jacob, and that is why he described the sons rather than give a prediction for them. He did reveal the future, however. The reason the Shechinah left is because predictions will not resolve problems. The Shechinah is our link to universal knowledge concerning the world we live in. If that link does not exist and the time has not come, there will be no prediction. Four hundred years ago, Rav Avraham Azulai predicted very clearly what would happen in the year 5760. The Zohar also occasionally makes a prediction, and we, too, strive for that connection. Without that connection, we do not know what the future will be.

The reason predictions do not work in everyday life is because there is nothing that can be done about what is predicted. What benefit is there for me to know the chaos that might await me in the future if I cannot do anything about it? The Zohar explains that Jacob provided us with a solution so we can control events, which we do every Rosh Chodesh (New Moon) celebration on the first day of the astrological month so we can control the course of the coming month. In this reading we are given the opportunity to gain control over all the months of the year, so we can control our destiny and finally remove chaos from this universe.

Many times, the Torah and the Zohar guarantee a life filled with abundance when we perform the precepts of the Bible. And yet the past 3,400 years have contained nothing but chaos. The precepts are not what is most crucial. Human dignity is the key. The precepts are only supposed to bring us to a consciousness of treating others with greater human dignity.

Vayechi is the final portion of the seed level, which is the Book of Beresheet. With this knowledge and energy we can put into the physical world all the tools that have been made available in the Book of Beresheet, which is the non-physical, non-observable seed level.

The Mystery of the Blessings

The Bible does not say Jacob called the children so he could bless them. It very clearly states "gather together and I will tell you that which shall occur to you." Yet there is no mention at all of what will occur. When we examine the blessings Jacob gave to all twelve children, none of them can be understood literally. Thus what is the real meaning here? We are discussing one or two lines that are mentioned in the Bible; the rest is totally incomprehensible commentary.

To understand the complexity of this section, we must turn again to the Zohar. The anti-kabbalists have been so successful, pursuing a good plan to keep us in the dark for 3,400 years. The anti-kabbalist tells us the Bible is too profound for us to understand, and that they are the only ones to help us with our daily pain and suffering. But, as we have learned from the Zohar, here there is no such word as blessing. In the translations it does not say "blessing," it says Jacob "blessed" his sons. Forgetting the idea of Jacob sharing information about the future, this is difficult to comprehend. Did Jacob not bless the children here? The Zohar says he did not. How then does this concern you and me?

For 3,400 years, we have not seen any lessening of pain, suffering, war or holocausts. Then what is meant by blessing here? We have understood from the Zohar that each and every single month has its own unique and particular energy, which is infused into the entire universe. Unfortunately, together with this energy come those creatures that want to suck the energy. They want Light. We know that Satan and his entire armada do not have any Light of their own. They commandeer Light. But they can only nourish themselves with what Light is available from us or the universe. They nourish themselves from this Light that is available each and every month.

When we connect to the combinations of words in a literal way, these have no significance, no meaning—they are simply arbitrary interpretations of each blessing. There is no room for interpretation, unless it is the Zohar's interpretation. The Zohar provides the tools and the technology by which we human beings can make the connection—we, who do not otherwise possess the physical wherewithal to connect with and link to this energy that appears each and every single month. Furthermore, these connections also enable us to prevent Satan and his cohorts from draining this energy, since we are influenced by such negativity and they have countless methods of infiltrating our systems.

What we have today is a great opportunity, whether we understand the codes we are being provided with or not. Vayechi is such a small portion, only 85 verses, yet it is interpreted by 300 pages of Zohar. In fact, the previous portion of Vayigash gets only 44 pages of interpretation from the Zohar. This is only to indicate that what is less is more, and what is more is less.

Therefore, while we do not understand one single word of what these, for lack of a better word, "blessings" to the children consist of, what we do know from the Zohar is that they concern Jacob sharing the future with his children, and similarly with us, today. He shared with us this technology we do not understand, and we do not have to understand. It is no different than when we are stuck and do not know the answer and can call upon the Light. We can say the Ana Beko'ach, which has absolutely no literal meaning, yet it is our technology.

These are the tools that provide us with an opportunity to tap into the awesome power that normally, with our rational minds, we would never be able to access. This is why people come to the Kabbalah Centres, to project themselves into the future; to learn the technology, to learn how to use the tools. There are 300 pages of Zohar that, even if one does not understand them, simply by scanning the words we can access the meaning of the technology of this portion. Today, the Zohar is also available in an English translation.

29 Then he gave them these instructions: "I am about to be gathered to my people. Bury me with my fathers in the cave in the field of Ephron the Hittite, 30 the cave in the field of Machpelah, near Mamre in Canaan, which Abraham bought as a burial place from Ephron the Hittite, along with the field. 31 There Abraham and his wife Sarah were buried, there Isaac and his wife Rebecca were buried, and there I buried Leah. 32 The field and the cave in it were bought from the Hittites." 33 When Jacob had finished giving instructions to his sons, he drew his feet up into the bed, breathed his last, and was gathered to his people.

Jacob and Immortality

The Bible says here that Jacob breathed his last breath and was gathered to his people—but the Zohar says Jacob did not die. We know Israel (Jacob) never died, for the power of Zeir Anpin is what Israel represents, so it cannot die. The Bible says Jacob was put in the Cave of Machpela at Hebron, yet the Zohar discusses immortality. The Zohar says Jacob wanted to tell his sons about the coming of the Messiah (*Mashiach*), the Final Redemption. Time, space, and motion were not a reality for him; prophecy means seeing the past and the future as today. After 2,000 years, scientists are finally beginning to comprehend this Zoharic concept. They just do not know how to put this knowledge to practical use yet. They say that soon we will be able to see through matter. If I flip a coin and cover it with my hand, is it heads or tails? Is it not already known which it is? When I take my hand away and see the coin, did I make it suddenly appear there? No, the coin is either heads or tails beneath my hand. Science knows we should be able to predict what is under my hand, but the scientists have yet to make it a reality.

We know that with the help of the Ana Beko'ach we can get rid of the Satan and all the obstacles that block us from seeing reality—especially the first letters of each word in the first line of the Ana Beko'ach, which are *Alef, Bet, Gimel, Yud, Taf, Tzadik*. This sequence of first letters removes all the blockages and negative influences from the physical world of the Tree of Knowledge Reality.

Years ago, we began to speak about immortality, the end of death, and many of the people who are against the Centres, especially those in the Orthodox community, said we were doing it as a gimmick to attract people—this being the means that have allowed us to grow to have the largest congregations of all synagogues in the world. Ten years ago, no one was talking about immortality. It was not a concept anyone thought possible. Not even science had conceived of the idea. But the prophets talked about it thousands of years ago: *bila hamavet laNetzach* (death will be swallowed up for eternity).

Religious leaders said the average Jew could not understand concepts like immortality, and that people had to learn only through rabbis. They did not feel people should be introduced to such ideas. Instead they kept the people in a state of ignorance. Here we educate people, and let them know about these concepts and about using the tools to achieve higher consciousness. The mainstream world calls us a cult. Is a cult, not a group, that tells their people to believe only what the cult leaders say? Is a cult, not a group, where the leaders want to keep people uneducated? We tell people to be educated and get more information, and yet we are still called a cult? This tells me that the Kabbalah Centres are on the right path. They say there is nothing to this portion but I say there is everything in this portion.

The Zohar says Jacob did not die, and it also communicates other revelations that apparently many rabbis do not want the people to know; this is also why some people even want to burn the Zohar! Death is an illusion. We think because we do not see a person after death that, therefore, they are no more. Perhaps the so-called dead are looking up from the other side and thinking that we here are the ones who are dead because they do not see us? As long as we consider death to be a reality, which really means they are simply no longer visible, then death is death. We need to know that immortality is already a reality; immortality is here, it is just covered like the coin in my hand.

This portion provides us with the energy of Jacob, whose time was up, but rather than die he expired (*vayigva*)—a word which is often not properly translated. This is the energy we can obtain from the reading—that death will indeed take a long vacation. The Zohar further explains that death is indeed an illusion. The energy we can receive from this reading is that of eternal life—immortality.

In Vayechi, Jacob reveals everything to the twelve sons (who are the twelve tribes, and also the twelve zodiacal signs), and by this we overcome the effects of the twelve months and go beyond physicality. Jacob revealed prophecy to his sons and to the twelve tribes through the blessings he gave them. Jacob's prophecy did not come in a dream and it did not come while he was in Israel—it came to him in Egypt. This is why the Bible tells us Jacob lived seventeen years in Egypt. It was the revelation of that which was concealed. The Zohar says Satan has headquarters in a few places around the world—and one of those places is Egypt. Israel is not one of the places in which Satan has headquarters. This is why Jacob and Moses had such great prophecy in Egypt. They could reveal that which was concealed by Satan.

We all have the ability to have prophecy but we must first eliminate the illusion. Religious leaders call this nonsense, asking people by what right they think they can know the future. These leaders insist that to do so one needs to be a great man—in other words, a rabbi.

Prophecy is the power to eliminate the negative influence of the physical realm. People often ask how they can gain prophecy, the ability to see into the future. But there is no educational institution in which you can learn how to become a prophet. We cannot teach prophecy; to have prophecy is to learn how to remove the obstacles that keep reality hidden. Consider the disease of cancer. It is where chaos reigns supreme in the physical reality. We should be able to remove the obstacles and illusions first, and thereby only then be able to eliminate the cancer.

Beresheet 50:1 Joseph threw himself upon his father and wept over him and kissed him. 2 Then Joseph directed the physicians in his service to embalm his father Israel. So the physicians embalmed him, 3 taking a full forty days, for that was the time required for embalming. And the Egyptians mourned for him seventy days.

Galut and Correction

This portion is about the aspect of immortality. Although scripture says Jacob died, Jacob did not die. Whatever is stated in the Bible is not necessarily fact, but rather it is the gateway through which we can reach and understand the inner secrets of the Zohar and, more importantly, immortality.

It is very strange that after Vayechi we immediately proceed to the Book of Shemot, which, as we have said previously, is not the exodus from Egypt because the Bible says the Israelites went into Egypt. Egypt is a code for *galut* (exile). What Egypt is referring to is our own "*galut*"—the pain and suffering we have to undergo.

The message is *mitzrayim* (מצרים), which means Egypt. The Israelites had no other language except Hebrew. When the Bible tells us Jacob went down to *mitzrayim*—entered into chaos—it is to help us understand that when we come into chaos this is part of a procedure, not the end of anything. The chaos we encounter is part of a process of correction in our lives; we owe our chaotic situations to our own actions. Yet if we have the consciousness that we want to get out of our own exile, how do we accomplish it? It is with the *Shemot*, with the Names. The Book of Shemot is full of the 72 Names of God. The word *Mitzrayim* is mentioned fifty times, which is not by chance—for those who study Kabbalah know that fifty means Jubilee, which, in turn, alludes to the Sefira of Binah. Wherever the word *Mitzrayim* is mentioned, it is there to teach us we can go into Egypt voluntarily to accept the necessary corrections. But why would we want to go into chaos voluntarily? If we could see the whole picture, however, we would be happy with this process.

4 When the days of mourning had passed, Joseph said to Pharaoh's court, "If I have found favor in your eyes, speak to Pharaoh for me. Tell him 5 my father made me swear an oath and said, 'I am about to die; bury me in the tomb I dug for myself in the land of Canaan.' Now let me go up and bury my father; then I will return." 6 Pharaoh said, "Go up and bury your father, as he made you swear to do." 7 So Joseph went up to bury his father. All Pharaoh's officials accompanied him—the dignitaries of his court and all the dignitaries of Egypt, 8 besides all the members of Joseph's household and his brothers and those belonging to his father's household. Only their children and their flocks and herds were left in Goshen. 9 Chariots and horseman also went up with him. It was a very large company. 10 When they reached the threshing floor of Atad, near the Jordan, they lamented loudly and bitterly; and there Joseph observed a seven-day period of mourning for his father. 11 When the Canaanites who lived there saw the mourning at the threshing floor of Atad, they said, "The Egyptians are holding a solemn ceremony of mourning." That is why that place near the Jordan is called Abel Mizrayim. 12 So Jacob's sons did as he had commanded them: 13 They carried him to the land of Canaan and buried him in the cave in the field of Machpelah, near Mamre, which Abraham had bought as a burial place from Ephron the Hittite, along with the field.

14 After burying his father, Joseph returned to Egypt, together with his brothers and all the others who had gone with him to bury his father. 15 When Joseph's brothers saw that their father was dead, they said, "What if Joseph holds a grudge against us and pays us back for all the wrongs we did to him?" 16 So they sent word to Joseph, saying, "Your father left these instructions before he died, 17 'This is what you are to say to Joseph: I ask you to forgive your brothers the sins and the wrongs they committed in treating you so badly. Now please forgive the sins of the servants of the God of your father.'" When their message came to him, Joseph wept. 18 His brothers then came and threw themselves down before him. "We are your slaves," they said. 19 But Joseph said to them, "Do not be afraid. For am I in the place of God?

Jacob's Energy Protected Even the Egyptians

The Zohar asks that if Jacob knew the Israelites would remain in Egypt and go through the pain of exile, why did he not request to stay there himself? He could have prayed for his people. Why did he ask to be buried in the Cave of Machpela?

The power of Jacob was that his very presence brought together the highest intensity of negative energy, and ultimately overwhelmed it. The reason we want to hear the reading of Vayechi is because, for at least the week of this portion, we are united with Jacob, who was able to create harmony, not only for the Israelites but for all of humankind. Jacob created a condition where negativity could no longer become manifest. When all the Egyptians mourned him, it was because they knew that with his death they would no longer be under his protective shield, and thus negativity would return to their lives. And, indeed, with the plagues and the exodus of the Israelites, that was the way it turned out for them. The Egyptians were very highly attuned to spiritual matters—they were the world's foremost astrologers. King Solomon says they were people of wisdom. They understood much of what would happen in the future. It was a culture of a very high level of consciousness but they became corrupt.

When we read the Torah Scroll, we become part of Jacob's life—if, that is, we are conscious of what we want to receive. If we do not consider the interpretation of the Zohar with regard to the phrase "And Jacob lived in Egypt," then it is as if we call someone on the telephone but refuse to speak with them. We have done everything to make the connection but one element is missing: the communication. We can hear the reading of a valid Torah Scroll but if we do not know what we want to receive, we are just listening. The Zohar says that this by itself is not sufficient. Knowing what we want to obtain from the reading is a worthwhile benefit for each week.

"For Am I in the Place of God?"

Here we encounter another interesting point in this portion. It is clear, at least in Hebrew, that Joseph says, "For am I in the place of God?" Some translations do not even consider this phrase because why would he say that? We know each one of us is a part of God, and therefore we are like God. Joseph was trying to tell his brothers by saying "Am I in place of God?" that whether he was a slave, head of a household, in prison, or second-in-command to the Pharaoh, he knew he would always be alright. When we can tap into our Godly nature within, then no matter in what situation we find ourselves, things will work out well.

169

20 You intended to harm me, but God intended it for good to accomplish what is now being done, the saving of many lives. 21 So then, don't be afraid. I will provide for you and your children." And he reassured them and spoke kindly to them.

Joseph Did Not Seek Revenge

Joseph was in a position to treat his brothers like slaves as a revenge for them having sold him into slavery. Yet Joseph saw the big picture—he saw the Tree of Life. Joseph is Yesod, so, of course, he did not consider the possibility of losing his high level of consciousness for the mere satisfaction of revenge. He foresaw the chaos such an action would create. He knew that, as Joseph, he was the one who gathers in the good to himself so he can disseminate to all the Tree of Life energy.

22 Joseph stayed in Egypt, along with all his father's family. He lived a hundred and ten years, 23 and saw the third generation of Ephraim's children. Also the children of Machir, son of Manasseh, were placed at birth on Joseph's knees. 24 Then Joseph said to his brothers, "I am about to die. But God will surely come to your aid and take you up out of this land to the land he promised on oath to Abraham, Isaac, and Jacob." 25 And Joseph made the sons of Israel swear an oath and said, "God will surely come to your aid, and then you must carry my bones up from this place." 26 So Joseph died at the age of a hundred and ten. And after they embalmed him, he was placed in a coffin in Egypt.

The Value of the End of the Book of Beresheet

We have *chazak, chazak, chazak* at the end of this book. The word *chazak* means strength, which assists us to forge a strong connection to manifesting the energy of the whole book. The three *chazaks* together have the same numerical value as *Mem, Hei, Shin*—the 72 Names of God for Healing. Each *chazak* has the same numerical value as *Pei, Hei, Lamed*—the 72 Name of God for Victory Over Addictions.

Vayechi is Malchut. Malchut always signifies the manifestation of everything that preceded it. It is like the fruit of the tree. When a seed of that fruit is planted, the seed itself contains everything that will appear; yet the purpose of the seed is not for the beauty of the tree itself but for the fruit that appears on it. Vayechi has a very specific significance, since it relates to Malchut of Beresheet, the final manifestation of Keter (the crown or seed). Whenever Vayechi is read in the future, we must first be conscious of why and where it is located.

In this last portion of the Book of Beresheet, we have the prophecy of Jacob; and in the Book of Shemot we have the story of Moses with the Israelites in slavery in Egypt, and then the redemption from Egypt. In the Book of Beresheet, however, there is a concealment of miracles. Joseph was sold by his brothers into slavery and became head of the household of Potiphar. He was put in prison, yet soon he had control over it. He then rose to become second in command to Pharaoh himself. These are all miracles but they are concealed. In the Book of Shemot, (which correctly translated does not mean "Exodus" but rather "Names") all the miracles are revealed: the Ten Plagues, the Splitting of the Red Sea, the Revelation at Mount Sinai and the Burning Bush, to name just a few.

As a side note, Moses did not want to be a leader. He wanted to be a teacher, which is what the word rabbenu (from whence "rabbi" is derived) actually means.

Significance of 85 Verses

The kabbalists designated the length of each portion because they knew its inner significance. Vayechi contains 85 verses. The number 85 refers to the word *peh*, which means "mouth." According to the study of Kabbalah, we understand that each part of our body has a particular and unique energy. The eyes have their own energy; the ears have their own energy. When we harmonize all the parts within us, we create a symphony in our own system. Everything then works in unison like an orchestra, smoothly moving as one whole within the universe. The mouth is the Malchut of the head, which indicates to us that Vayechi has the power of Malchut. What is the power of Malchut? It is the ingathering of everything that preceded it. In this case, it is the ingathering of every other portion that preceded this particular portion.

As we have already learned, with the Five Books of Moses, the first book is Beresheet and the last book is Devarim; Beresheet is Keter and Devarim is Malchut. The code name Keter (which means Crown) is the seed. The Book of Beresheet contains every secret of the universe. This entire book provides us—as we proceed on with it each Shabbat—the understanding on a potential level, on a seed level, of all the knowledge of the universe and also of ourselves, so we can be in a better position to organize our personal rhythm to match the rhythm of the entire universe.

We need to harmonize ourselves with all that is around us and not create conflict within the universe. The reason Vayechi is so significant is that those who may have missed one reading now have the opportunity of ingathering all that was revealed from the previous readings. What happens if you have not missed any of the preceding portions? Some might say such people do not have to be present for the reading of Vayechi because it is only Malchut—the whole is the sum of its parts. But according to Kabbalah it is known that the whole is another entity altogether. Why would the whole be more than the sum of its parts? When each part is placed together, and not read as a separate portion then the entire book has been brought into harmony. All the profound knowledge of the universe is brought into harmony because the Book of Beresheet contains everything that exists in this universe and beyond.

The Zohar says there are more than ten planets. In fact, there are 250,000 planets, and, as soul entities, we travel to all of these planets. We only discuss ten of them, however. In the Ana Beko'ach, we concentrate on the seven that directly affect us—Sun, Moon, Mercury, Mars, Venus, Jupiter, and Saturn.

As we read the Bible each week, we absorb information, consciously or unconsciously. Remember, our 99 percent is the unconscious part of our being, a part which many of us are not even aware exists. We place so much emphasis on the one percent rational consciousness—which I call the Satan—and pretty much ignore the other 99 percent. This 99 percent is the root of what Kabbalah is really all about.

Conclusion

With Vayechi, we have the conclusion, the summation, the sum of all its parts—the entire harmonious symphony of all the universe's knowledge. When I quote the Zohar, I am sharing 25th century physics. It is presented here as prophecy, which means I cannot necessarily see or understand it right now; but we are privy to this invaluable wisdom, which is capable of transforming our lives—and the reason it can do this is because we are connected to the whole and not limited by the parts. We are not limited by each year's progression of information to continually improve our lives. Let us not forget to appreciate this gift, because in the one percent of our consciousness we are smug and self-satisfied.

With this portion, we can obtain the energy of all the previous portions combined. This is a huge merit. It is like a narrative where we can return at will to parts we have missed. Even if we have neglected to connect to one of the readings, we are fortunate to have the opportunity with the portion of Vayechi to receive everything.

It is practically impossible to get back to the seed level after the Book of Beresheet. Either you have grasped it or you have not.

The Book of Shemot is about slavery. In the Book of Shemot we receive the 72 Names of God, and each one can help us to eliminate a certain aspect of chaos. The meditation on 72 Names (*Shemot*) is the only way whereby we may eliminate chaos. But nonetheless we are still obliged to undergo a process. The Book of Beresheet is concerned with the prevention of slavery and chaos. In the Book of Beresheet there is no process; we are at the seed level.

Only about three percent of the people reading this will understand it. Millions of people have come through the doors of Kabbalah Centres and taken classes, but to most it was only information—it went in one ear and out the other. The prime reason people do not continue with Kabbalah, even after they have been in a Kabbalah Centre for a while, is because to them it is just information. If Kabbalah does not become part of us, then there is no benefit. We earn the Light through our spiritual work. When we say *Chazak, Chazak, Chazak, Venitchazek* we are taking this power and injecting it into the future—for ourselves and also for the entire world, thereby closing the doors to chaos in our lives.

About the Centres

Kabbalah is the deepest and most hidden meaning of the Torah or Bible. Through the ultimate knowledge and mystical practices of Kabbalah, one can reach the highest spiritual levels attainable. Although many people rely on belief, faith, and dogmas in pursuing the meaning of life, Kabbalists seek a spiritual connection with the Creator and the forces of the Creator, so that the strange becomes familiar, and faith becomes knowledge.

Throughout history, those who knew and practiced the Kabbalah were extremely careful in their dissemination of the knowledge because they knew the masses of mankind had not yet prepared for the ultimate truth of existence. Today, kabbalists know that it is not only proper but necessary to make the Kabbalah available to all who seek it.

The Research Centre of Kabbalah is an independent, non-profit institute founded in Israel in 1922. The Centre provides research, information, and assistance to those who seek the insights of Kabbalah. The Centre offers public lectures, classes, seminars, and excursions to mystical sites at branches in Israel and in the United States. Branches have been opened in Mexico, Montreal, Toronto, Paris, Hong Kong, and Taiwan.

Our courses and materials deal with the Zoharic understanding of each weekly portion of the Torah. Every facet of life is covered and other dimensions, hithertofore unknown, provide a deeper connection to a superior reality. Three important beginner courses cover such aspects as: Time, Space and Motion; Reincarnation, Marriage, Divorce; Kabbalistic Meditation; Limitation of the Five Senses; Illusion-Reality; Four Phases; Male and Female, Death, Sleep, Dreams; Food; and Shabbat.

Thousands of people have benefited from the Centre's activities, and the Centre's publishing of kabbalistic material continues to be the most comprehensive of its kind in the world, including translations in English, Hebrew, Russian, German, Portuguese, French, Spanish, Farsi (Persian).

Kabbalah can provide one with the true meaning of their being and the knowledge necessary for their ultimate benefit. It can show one spirituality that is beyond belief. The Research Centre of Kabbalah will continue to make available the Kabbalah to all those who seek it.

—Rav Berg, 1984

About The Zohar

The Zohar, the basic source of the Kabbalah, was authored two thousand years ago by Rabbi Shimon bar Yochai while hiding from the Romans in a cave in Peki'in for 13 years. It was later brought to light by Rabbi Moses de Leon in Spain, and further revealed through the Safed Kabbalists and the Lurianic system of Kabbalah.

The programs of the Research Centre of Kabbalah have been established to provide opportunities for learning, teaching, research, and demonstration of specialized knowledge drawn from the ageless wisdom of the Zohar and the Jewish sages. Long kept from the masses, today this knowledge of the Zohar and Kabbalah should be shared by all who seek to understand the deeper meaning of this spiritual heritage, and a deeper and more profound meaning of life. Modern science is only beginning to discover what our sages veiled in symbolism. This knowledge is of a very practical nature and can be applied daily for the betterment of our lives and of humankind.

Darkness cannot prevail in the presence of Light. Even a darkened room must respond to the lighting of a candle. As we share this moment together we are beginning to witness, and indeed some of us are already participating in, a people's revolution of enlightenment. The darkened clouds of strife and conflict will make their presence felt only as long as the Eternal Light remains concealed.

The Zohar now remains an ultimate, if not the only, solution to infusing the cosmos with the revealed Lightforce of the Creator. The Zohar is not a book about religion. Rather, the Zohar is concerned with the relationship between the unseen forces of the cosmos, the Lightforce, and the impact on humanity.

The Zohar promises that with the ushering in of the Age of Aquarius, the cosmos will become readily accessible to human understanding. It states that in the days of the Messiah "there will no longer be the necessity for one to request of his neighbor, teach me wisdom." (Zohar, Naso 9:65) "One day, they will no longer teach every man his neighbor and every man his brother, saying know the Lord. For they shall all know Me, from the youngest to the oldest of them." (Jeremiah 31:34)

We can, and must, regain dominion of our lives and environment. To achieve this objective, the Zohar provides us with an opportunity to transcend the crushing weight of universal negativity.

The daily perusing of the Zohar, without any attempt at translation or understanding will fill our consciousness with the Light, improving our well-being, and influencing all in our environment toward positive attitudes. Even the scanning of the Zohar by those unfamiliar with the Hebrew *Alef Bet* will accomplish the same result.

The connection that we establish through scanning the Zohar is one of unity with the Light of the Creator. The letters, even if we do not consciously know Hebrew or Aramaic, are the channels through which the connection is made and can be likened to dialing the right telephone number or typing in the right codes to run a computer program. The connection is established at the metaphysical level of our being and radiates into our physical plane of existence. But first there is the prerequisite of metaphysical "fixing." We have to consciously, through positive thought and actions, permit the immense power of the Zohar to radiate love, harmony, and peace into our lives for us to share with all humanity and the universe.

As we enter the years ahead, the Zohar will continue to be a people's book, striking a sympathetic chord in the hearts and minds of those who long for peace, truth, and relief from suffering. In the face of crises and catastrophe, the Zohar has the ability to resolve agonizing human afflictions by restoring each individual's relationship with the Lightforce of the Creator.

—Rav Berg, 1984

Kabbalah Centre Books

72 Names of God, The: Technology for the Soul

72 Names of God for Kids, The: A Treasury of Timeless Wisdom

72 Names of God Meditation Book, The

And You Shall Choose Life: An Essay on Kabbalah, the Purpose of Life, and Our True Spiritual Work

Angel Intelligence: How Your Consciousness Determines Which Angels Come Into Your Life

AstrologiK: Kabbalistic Astrology Guide for Children

Becoming Like God: Kabbalah and Our Ultimate Destiny

Beloved of My Soul: Letters of Our Master and Teacher Rav Yehuda Tzvi Brandwein to His Beloved Student Kabbalist Rav Berg

Consciousness and the Cosmos (previously Star Connection)

Days of Connection: A Guide to Kabbalah's Holidays and New Moons

Days of Power Part 1

Days of Power Part 2

Dialing God: Daily Connection Book

Education of a Kabbalist

Energy of the Hebrew Letters, The (previously Power of the Aleph Beth Vols. 1 and 2)

Fear is Not an Option

Finding the Light Through the Darkness: Inspirational Lessons Rooted in the Bible and the Zohar

God Wears Lipstick: Kabbalah for Women

Holy Grail, The: A Manifesto on the Zohar

If You Don't Like Your Life, Change It!: Using Kabbalah to Rewrite the Movie of Your Life

Immortality: The Inevitability of Eternal Life

Kabbalah Connection, The: Preparing the Soul For Pesach

Kabbalah for the Layman

Kabbalah Method, The: The Bridge Between Science and the Soul, Physics and Fulfillment, Quantum and the Creator

Kabbalah on the Sabbath: Elevating Our Soul to the Light

Kabbalah: The Power To Change Everything

Kabbalistic Astrology: And the Meaning of Our Lives

Kabbalistic Bible: Genesis

Kabbalistic Bible: Exodus

Kabbalistic Bible: Leviticus

Kabbalistic Bible: Numbers

Kabbalistic Bible: Deuteronomy

Light of Wisdom: On Wisdom, Life, and Eternity

Miracles, Mysteries, and Prayer Volume 1

Miracles, Mysteries, and Prayer Volume 2

Nano: Technology of Mind over Matter

Navigating The Universe: A Roadmap for Understanding the Cosmic Influences that Shape Our Lives (previously Time Zones)

On World Peace: Two Essays by the Holy Kabbalist Rav Yehuda Ashlag

Path to the Light: Decoding the Bible with Kabbalah: Book of Beresheet Volume 1

Path to the Light: Decoding the Bible with Kabbalah: Book of Beresheet Volume 2

Path to the Light: Decoding the Bible with Kabbalah: Book of Beresheet Volume 3

Prayer of the Kabbalist, The: The 42-Letter Name of God

Power of Kabbalah, The: 13 Principles to Overcome Challenges and Achieve Fulfillment

Rebooting: Defeating Depression with the Power of Kabbalah

Satan: An Autobiography

Secret, The: Unlocking the Source of Joy & Fulfillment

Secrets of the Bible: Teachings from Kabbalistic Masters

Secrets of the Zohar: Stories and Meditations to Awaken the Heart

Simple Light: Wisdom from a Woman's Heart

Shabbat Connections

Taming Chaos: Harnessing the Secret Codes of the Universe to Make Sense of Our Lives

Thought of Creation, The: On the Individual, Humanity, and Their Ultimate Perfection

To Be Continued: Reincarnation & the Purpose of Our Lives

To the Power of One

True Prosperity: How to Have Everything

Vokabbalahry: Words of Wisdom for Kids to Live By

Way Of The Kabbalist, The: A User's Guide to Technology for the Soul

Well of Life: Kabbalistic Wisdom from a Depth of Knowledge

Wheels of a Soul: Kabbalah and Reincarnation

Wisdom of Truth, The: 12 Essays by the Holy Kabbalist Rav Yehuda Ashlag

Zohar, The

BOOKS AVAILABLE AT
WWW. KABBALAH.COM/STORE
AND KABBALAH CENTRES AROUND THE WORLD